Human Trafficking

Other Books of Related Interest

Opposing Viewpoints Series

LGBTQIA+ Rights
Peoples on the Move: The Immigration Crisis
Reproductive Rights

At Issue Series

Genocide
Money Laundering
Policing in America

Current Controversies Series

Cryptocurrencies and Blockchain Technology
The Dark Web
Immigration, Asylum, and Sanctuary Cities

> “Congress shall make no law … abridging the freedom of speech, or of the press.”
>
> *First Amendment to the U.S. Constitution*

The basic foundation of our democracy is the First Amendment guarantee of freedom of expression. The Opposing Viewpoints series is dedicated to the concept of this basic freedom and the idea that it is more important to practice it than to enshrine it.

Human Trafficking

Lisa Idzikowski, Book Editor

Published in 2023 by Greenhaven Publishing, LLC
2544 Clinton Street,
Buffalo NY 14224

First Edition

Cover image: structuresxx/Shutterstock.com

Library of Congress CataloginginPublication Data

Names: Idzikowski, Lisa, editor.
Title: Human trafficking / Lisa Idzikowski, book editor.
Description: First Edition. | Buffalo, NY : Greenhaven Publishing, 2023. | Series: Opposing viewpoints | Includes bibliographical references and index. | Audience: Grades 10-12.
Identifiers: LCCN 2022054735 | ISBN 9781534509207 (library binding) | ISBN 9781534509191 (paperback)
Subjects: LCSH: Human trafficking--Juvenile literature.
Classification: LCC HQ281 .H8322 2023 | DDC 364.15/51--dc23/eng/20221110
LC record available at https://lccn.loc.gov/2022054735

Manufactured in the United States of America

Website: http://greenhavenpublishing.com

Contents

Chapter 4: Can Human Trafficking Be Prevented?

The Importance of Opposing Viewpoints

Perhaps every generation experiences a period in time in which the populace seems especially polarized, starkly divided on the important issues of the day and gravitating toward the far ends of the political spectrum and away from a consensus-facilitating middle ground. The world that today's students are growing up in and that they will soon enter into as active and engaged citizens is deeply fragmented in just this way. Issues relating to terrorism, immigration, women's rights, minority rights, race relations, health care, taxation, wealth and poverty, the environment, policing, military intervention, the proper role of government—in some ways, perennial issues that are freshly and uniquely urgent and vital with each new generation—are currently roiling the world.

If we are to foster a knowledgeable, responsible, active, and engaged citizenry among today's youth, we must provide them with the intellectual, interpretive, and critical-thinking tools and experience necessary to make sense of the world around them and of the all-important debates and arguments that inform it. After all, the outcome of these debates will in large measure determine the future course, prospects, and outcomes of the world and its peoples, particularly its youth. If they are to become successful members of society and productive and informed citizens, students need to learn how to evaluate the strengths and weaknesses of someone else's arguments, how to sift fact from opinion and fallacy, and how to test the relative merits and validity of their own opinions against the known facts and the best possible available information. The landmark series Opposing Viewpoints has been providing students with just such critical-thinking skills and exposure to the debates surrounding society's most urgent contemporary issues for many years, and it continues to serve this essential role with undiminished commitment, care, and rigor.

The key to the series's success in achieving its goal of sharpening students' critical-thinking and analytic skills resides in its title—

Opposing Viewpoints. In every intriguing, compelling, and engaging volume of this series, readers are presented with the widest possible spectrum of distinct viewpoints, expert opinions, and informed argumentation and commentary, supplied by some of today's leading academics, thinkers, analysts, politicians, policy makers, economists, activists, change agents, and advocates. Every opinion and argument anthologized here is presented objectively and accorded respect. There is no editorializing in any introductory text or in the arrangement and order of the pieces. No piece is included as a "straw man," an easy ideological target for cheap point-scoring. As wide and inclusive a range of viewpoints as possible is offered, with no privileging of one particular political ideology or cultural perspective over another. It is left to each individual reader to evaluate the relative merits of each argument—as he or she sees it, and with the use of ever-growing critical-thinking skills—and grapple with his or her own assumptions, beliefs, and perspectives to determine how convincing or successful any given argument is and how the reader's own stance on the issue may be modified or altered in response to it.

This process is facilitated and supported by volume, chapter, and selection introductions that provide readers with the essential context they need to begin engaging with the spotlighted issues, with the debates surrounding them, and with their own perhaps shifting or nascent opinions on them. In addition, guided reading and discussion questions encourage readers to determine the authors' point of view and purpose, interrogate and analyze the various arguments and their rhetoric and structure, evaluate the arguments' strengths and weaknesses, test their claims against available facts and evidence, judge the validity of the reasoning, and bring into clearer, sharper focus the reader's own beliefs and conclusions and how they may differ from or align with those in the collection or those of their classmates.

Research has shown that reading comprehension skills improve dramatically when students are provided with compelling, intriguing, and relevant "discussable" texts. The subject matter of these collections could not be more compelling, intriguing, or urgently relevant to today's students and the world they are poised to inherit. The anthologized articles and the reading and discussion questions that are included with them also provide the basis for stimulating, lively, and passionate classroom debates. Students who are compelled to anticipate objections to their own argument and identify the flaws in those of an opponent read more carefully, think more critically, and steep themselves in relevant context, facts, and information more thoroughly. In short, using discussable text of the kind provided by every single volume in the Opposing Viewpoints series encourages close reading, facilitates reading comprehension, fosters research, strengthens critical thinking, and greatly enlivens and energizes classroom discussion and participation. The entire learning process is deepened, extended, and strengthened.

For all of these reasons, Opposing Viewpoints continues to be exactly the right resource at exactly the right time—when we most need to provide readers with the critical-thinking tools and skills that will not only serve them well in school but also in their careers and their daily lives as decision-making family members, community members, and citizens. This series encourages respectful engagement with and analysis of opposing viewpoints and fosters a resulting increase in the strength and rigor of one's own opinions and stances. As such, it helps make readers "future ready," and that readiness will pay rich dividends for the readers themselves, for the citizenry, for our society, and for the world at large.

Introduction

> *"Trafficking victims are deceived by false promises of love, a good job, or a stable life and are lured or forced into situations where they are made to work under deplorable conditions with little or no pay."*
>
> *–United States Department of Justice*

Human trafficking is by no means a new crime—it has been happening for centuries. What is rather new, however, is the global effort to curtail it, which began in the mid-1990s. Both the United States, with the Trafficking Victims Protection Act of 2000, and the United Nations, with the Protocol to Prevent, Suppress, and Punish Trafficking in Persons, Especially Women and Children, have actively sought to prevent and limit this highly organized criminal activity.

According to *Merriam-Webster,* the term "human trafficking" was first used in 1904 and is defined as an "organized criminal activity in which human beings are treated as possessions to be controlled and exploited (as by being forced into prostitution or involuntary labor)."[1] The United Nations, on the other hand defines human trafficking as

> the recruitment, transportation, transfer, harbouring or receipt of people through force, fraud or deception, with the aim of exploiting them for profit. Men, women and children of all ages and from all backgrounds can become victims of this crime, which occurs in every region of the world.[2]

In July of 2021, U.S. Secretary of State Antony Blinken said that human trafficking is "a global crisis, it's an enormous source of human suffering," and estimated that almost 25 million people—including many children—are trafficking victims.[3] The United States and other nations use the "3P" paradigm—prosecution, protection, and prevention—to organize attempts to combat trafficking. It's probably safe to say that most people would agree that stopping trafficking is a worthy goal. However, experts tend to agree that it is difficult to quantify whether trafficking is a growing problem or has simply been underreported in the past. There are also many misunderstandings about what human trafficking is and how it occurs that stand in the way of effectively preventing it.

According to the National Human Trafficking Hotline, there are several prevailing myths surrounding the crime of human trafficking.[4] These myths make it difficult to get a sense of the scope of the issue and are obstacles to stopping it. One myth is that traffickers target victims they do not know. Another myth states that trafficking in labor is only a problem in developing countries, not in countries like the United States. Another harmful belief is that trafficking victims could have prevented their situation, and that people who are trafficked choose to put themselves in these dangerous and harmful positions. These are not the only myths surrounding human trafficking, but just a few that will be addressed in the viewpoints in this book.

This volume examines several important questions about human trafficking from a wide range of perspectives. What is human trafficking? What are the financial aspects of the crime? Does technology play a role in trafficking? How can governments and organizations help prevent this criminal enterprise? The expert viewpoints presented in this book will allow readers to contemplate and understand the timely questions surrounding the issue of human trafficking by exploring *Opposing Viewpoints: Human Trafficking*, which sheds light on this ongoing contemporary issue.

Notes

1. "Human Trafficking," *Merriam-Webster*. https://www.merriam-webster.com/dictionary/human%20trafficking.
2. "Human Trafficking," UNODC. https://www.unodc.org/unodc/en/human-Trafficking/Human-Trafficking.html.
3. Matthew Lee, "U.S. hits 17 nations for not combatting human trafficking," PBS, July 1, 2021. https://www.pbs.org/newshour/politics/u-s-hits-17-nations-for-not-combating-human-trafficking.
4. "Human Trafficking: Myths and Facts," National Human Trafficking Hotline. https://humantraffickinghotline.org/what-human-trafficking/myths-misconceptions.

Chapter 1

What Causes Human Trafficking Today?

Chapter Preface

Is human trafficking a topic on people's minds? What is it, and how common is it? Many people believe a number of myths about human trafficking that make it even more difficult to answer these questions: that it doesn't happen in the United States and other developed countries; that victims could leave if they wanted, or not get involved in the first place if they were careful; that only women and girls are caught up in this situation. In reality, human trafficking happens around the world, to many individuals of all genders who typically cannot just walk away from a bad situation.

One major question that troubles both experts and the public is what causes this illegal activity. According to human trafficking experts, this is a very complex question. Unfortunately, but maybe not surprisingly, this illicit industry is monetarily lucrative, which makes it attractive to individuals and groups already committing other illegal activities, including certain gangs that have ramped up their involvement in trafficking.

The viewpoints in this chapter analyze, describe, and expand on the question of what human trafficking is and how it occurs in contemporary society. The authors provide definitions of this crime and answer key questions surrounding the issue. Can the public help in any way to prevent trafficking from occurring? Are governments responsible for providing relief to victims? Is human trafficking an easily solved problem? Practical advice and information is also provided by the U.S. State Department, which provides insight into how people may protect themselves from becoming victims of trafficking. Reading and thinking about the viewpoints in this chapter will provide a foundational understanding on the issue of human trafficking.

Viewpoint 1

"While there's still a great deal that is unknown about sex trafficking, research studies and nonprofits have been able to gather telling data on this industry's victims and perpetrators."

What Is Sex Trafficking and How Does It Occur in the United States?

Monti Datta

In this viewpoint by Monti Datta, he explains that in order to prevent sex trafficking in the U.S., it's important to understand what it is and how it takes place today. Sex trafficking often takes place in illicit massage parlors, hotels and motels, and residential brothels, and these are often in impoverished neighborhoods near interstate highways and major urban centers. Victims are often runaway and homeless youth, and a significant percentage are LGBTQIA+. There are many different types of traffickers, and many different types of men purchase commercial sex, which makes it difficult to reach a consensus about who or what to look out for. Often the traffickers have complicated emotions about their work and the people they traffic, and may even believe they are protecting their victims. However, Datta asserts that better data collection will help in the fight against trafficking, along

"4 questions answered on sex trafficking in the US," Monti Datta, The Conversation, July 9, 2019. https://theconversation.com/4-questions-answered-on-sex-trafficking-in-the-us-120098. Licensed under CC BY 4.0 International.

with projects that involve training employees in the hospitality and trucking industries to identify trafficking. Monti Datta is an associate professor of political science at the University of Richmond.

As you read, consider the following questions:

1. How does the federal government define sex trafficking, according to this viewpoint?
2. What are some of the risk factors for sex trafficking listed in this viewpoint.
3. According to research referenced in this viewpoint, in what way do modern-day slaveholders have a complicated mindset?

The revelations about billionaire Jeffrey Epstein, who is accused of sex trafficking girls, paint a grim picture of sex trafficking in the U.S. The buying and selling of human beings is strong in America more than 150 years since the end of the Civil War.

Sex trafficking, as the federal government defines it, is "the recruitment, harboring, transportation, provision or obtaining of a person for the purpose of a commercial sex act" by means of "force, fraud, or coercion." This is a form of modern-day slavery.

Found in massage parlors, escort services, residential brothels and street prostitution, some might be victims for weeks and others for years.

As someone who studies human trafficking, I feel that it's important for the public to understand how it manifests in the U.S. today. While there's still a great deal that is unknown about sex trafficking, research studies and nonprofits have been able to gather telling data on this industry's victims and perpetrators.

1. Where Does Sex Trafficking Occur?

Sex trafficking tends to occur in motels and impoverished neighborhoods along the interstate highway system as well as in major urban centers. Some of the busiest corridors of the interstate include I-5 in the West, I-95 in the East and I-80, stretching from coast to coast.

The nonprofit Polaris operates the National Human Trafficking Hotline, which takes tips on sex and labor trafficking. Although the Polaris data are not from a random-sample survey, they shed light on types of sex trafficking in the U.S. In 2017, Polaris received more than 6,000 hotline tips about sex trafficking across America. Among these data, the top venues for sex trafficking included illicit massage parlors, hotels and motels, and residential brothels.

The National Association of Truck Stop Operators has partnered with the U.S. Department of Homeland Security's Blue Campaign. The National Association of Truck Stop Operators offers trainings to help truckers, truck stop owners and employees identify the signs of human trafficking, such as malnourishment, lack of eye contact and disorientation.

Hotel chains like Marriott are training their employees as well.

2. Who Are the Victims?

Reliable data on the number of sex trafficking victims in the U.S. are hard to come by.

In the U.S., studies show that most victims of sex trafficking are young women and girls. They are, on average, 19 years old.

Risk factors for sex trafficking include a history of child abuse, substance abuse, poverty, involvement in child protective services, involvement in juvenile detention and prior sexual exploitation.

Runaway and homeless youth are especially at risk for sex trafficking. A study conducted in Philadelphia, Washington, D.C. and Phoenix found that 14% of homeless youth identified themselves as victims of sex trafficking. Among these sex trafficking victims, 33% identified as LGBTQ.

A young person is more likely to meet her trafficker for the first time online rather than in person, due to the rise of social media.

3. Who Are the Traffickers and Johns?

Men who purchase commercial sex come from all walks of life.

One comparative study on men and their lifetime history of paying for sex found that 4.9% of men in Tampa, Florida, said they had ever paid for sex. Among those men who paid for sex in Tampa, men aged 41 to 70 were most likely to pay for sex, making up about 13% of the total.

Traffickers include mom-and-pop operations, crime rings, gangs and cartels. Sometimes, when a victim of sex trafficking has been groomed enough, she becomes "the bottom," helping her trafficker recruit other victims.

Research shows that modern-day slaveholders have a complicated mindset, condescending and paternalistic, not necessarily one of pure evil. Slaveholders can think they are doing a favor to the enslaved, by taking care of them, giving them food and shelter, and even "protecting" them from a world in which they would otherwise be disposable.

4. How Much Money Does the Commercial Sex Economy Generate?

A 2014 study of sex trafficking in seven major U.S. cities found that revenues from underground commercial sex ranged from US$39.9 million in Denver to $290 million in Atlanta.

Although many experts suspect that major sporting events, like the Super Bowl, might encourage the demand for commercial sex, preliminary research suggests the effect is negligible.

The breadth of sex trafficking in the U.S. has prompted federal responses. The FBI has organized Operation Cross Country, a collaboration of dozens of field offices and hundreds of local law enforcement organizations. In October 2017, Operation Cross Country XI conducted a nationwide sting leading to the freeing of 84 minors and the arrest of 120 traffickers.

With better data collection methods and a stronger national coordinated effort, the U.S. could eventually come closer to the day when modern slavery is no more.

Viewpoint 

> *"Traffickers look for people who are vulnerable and therefore easier to exploit."*

Many Factors Leave People Vulnerable to Human Trafficking

Province of British Columbia

In the following viewpoint, the government of the province of British Columbia and its Office to Combat Trafficking in Persons outline the situations that contribute to the practice of human trafficking. As the viewpoint describes, there are many different factors that typically enable traffickers to operate, including political, personal, social, and cultural variables. These include political instability, racism and colonialism, mental health and addiction, gender inequality, and gang involvement. The Office to Combat Trafficking is the first of its kind in Canada, and it is mandated to design British Columbia's response to domestic and international human trafficking.

As you read, consider the following questions:

1. According to the viewpoint, how does an online presence make one vulnerable to trafficking?
2. How does racism make someone a target for trafficking, as stated in this viewpoint?

"What Makes Someone Vulnerable to Human Trafficking?" British Columbia. Reprinted by permission.

3. Does gender make a difference in human trafficking according to this viewpoint?

Traffickers look for people who are vulnerable and therefore easier to exploit. The major factors—on both a societal and personal level—that cause or contribute to people being vulnerable to trafficking include:

Political Instability

War, civil unrest, political conflict, violence, lawlessness, and natural disasters create unstable conditions in which people may live in constant fear with limited options for survival or earning a living. Children may be separated from their families and left without parents or guardians to protect and advise them.

Political instability may also lead to forced migration where people flee from their homes in search of more stable or secure communities. However, they may instead end up homeless or in temporary settlements, unemployed and possibly unwanted by their host community, and without their familiar family and social networks. Traffickers take advantage of these desperate circumstances.

Poverty

Poverty creates despair. Traffickers specifically target poor and marginalized communities to offer vulnerable individuals false opportunities to improve their circumstances. Such people are more likely to take greater risks in order to provide for themselves and their families. Indigenous populations in many countries are often marginalized, which may result in their vulnerability to recruitment by traffickers.

Racism and the Legacy of Colonialism

Racism and colonialism contributed to the marginalization of people, particularly indigenous populations. People who experience racism face systemic barriers such as limited access to education, employment, housing, and credit. These continuous instances of discrimination place them at a higher risk of being trafficked.

Colonialism is the practice by which a nation acquires, controls, and rules a foreign territory for the purpose of exploiting its resources and people. The legacy of colonialism has continued to impact entire communities as people struggle to exercise their basic civil and human rights. Traffickers target people who are marginalized due to racism and colonialism, capitalizing on their vulnerabilities.

Gender Inequality

Gender inequality is the disparity between opportunities available to men and women based on gender. In many cultures, women are seen as less than men; are paid less for equal work; have fewer rights; less access to health, education, and property; are expected to be submissive to men; and are therefore vulnerable to recruitment by traffickers.

Addictions

Traffickers use substance dependency and addiction to keep control of the trafficked person. Some traffickers purposely supply drugs to vulnerable people to break down their resistance and coerce them into forced labour or sex. As a trafficked person becomes dependent on a particular substance, the trafficker uses that vulnerability to keep them in the cycle of abuse.

Mental Health

People with mental health issues face a variety of challenges including isolation, diminished capacity to consent or offer informed consent, and limited ability to assess risk and detect ill-intentions. Traffickers are skilled in detecting these vulnerabilities and manipulating them to their advantage.

Gang Involvement

For gangs, the exploitation of men, women, and children is lucrative and less risky than other trades such as weapons or drugs. Gang members recruit and exploit people in a variety of ways, including

The United Nations Researches the Causes of Human Trafficking

The 2020 UNODC Global Report on Trafficking in Persons (https://www.unodc.org/documents/data-and-analysis/tip/2021/GLOTiP_2020_15jan_web.pdf) is the fifth of its kind mandated by the General Assembly through the 2010 United Nations Global Plan of Action to Combat Trafficking in Persons. It covers 148 countries and provides an overview of patterns and flows of trafficking in persons at global, regional and national levels, based primarily on trafficking cases detected between 2016 and 2019. As UNODC has been systematically collecting data on trafficking in persons for more than a decade, trend information is presented for a broad range of indicators.

As with previous years, this edition of the Global Report on Trafficking in Persons presents a global picture of the patterns and flows of trafficking (Chapter 1), alongside detailed regional analyses (Chapter 6) and country profiles.

In addition, this Report provides four thematic chapters. Chapter 2 of the Report examines how poor socioeconomic conditions are used by traffickers to recruit and exploit victims. The third chapter expands on patterns of child trafficking and the roles that extreme poverty, social norms and familial backgrounds play in this form of trafficking. Then, the fourth chapter focuses on trafficking for forced labour and explores the specific economic sectors that are more vulnerable to trafficking. Finally, the fifth chapter presents emerging patterns on internet technologies that are used by traffickers to facilitate recruitment and exploitation.

"Trafficking in Persons," United Nations Office On Drugs and Crime (UNODC).

sexual exploitation, street begging, street vending, petty crime, and the manufacture and transportation of drugs. Gangs may also coerce their own members and peripheral associates to commit crimes, provide services and labour, and other activities against their will. Females can be exploited through gang involvement by entering as a girlfriend of a gang member, and then being sold within or outside the gang for sexual acts. Often youth are born into gang-involved families and there is the expectation that they will contribute to the family business in any way the gang deems fit.

Online Vulnerability

Traffickers maintain an online presence to lure vulnerable adults and children with the goal of meeting them in person, to take and circulate explicit photos, and to coerce an individual to comply with their demands. Traffickers often keep compromising photos or video of the people they are exploiting to further their control—they may threaten to publish these images online, or send them to the family and friends of the trafficked person.

VIEWPOINT 3

> *"The U.N. seems to be getting much better at estimating global slavery. But because the survey techniques are improving over time, it is impossible to make comparisons."*

Human Trafficking Has Always Existed, but Estimates of Its Scope Are Getting More Accurate

Monti Datta

According to a 2022 report from the United Nations, there are approximately 50 million people around the world who are forced into labor or marriage, both of which are defined as forms of enslavement by the United Nations. This figure is a significant increase from the 2017 estimates, which predicted that 40 million people were enslaved. However, this is likely because estimates are becoming more accurate due to improved data collection and analysis techniques. By offering more accurate estimates on how many people are trapped in slavery and human trafficking, organizations can encourage governments around the world to take action. Monti Datta is an associate professor of political science at the University of Richmond.

"U.N. slavery estimate raises questions: Are 50 million people really enslaved today?" by Monti Datta, The Conversation, September 29, 2022. https://theconversation.com/un-slavery-estimate-raises-question-are-50-million-people-really-enslaved-today-190882.

As you read, consider the following questions:

1. According to this viewpoint, what is considered forced labor?
2. What countries and regions are noted in this viewpoint as having a large amount of forced labor caused by poverty?
3. According to Datta, what makes it difficult to assess or replicate the United Nation's findings?

According to the United Nations, about 50 million people are enslaved worldwide.

The report, released Sept. 12, 2022, by the U.N.'s International Labor Organization, the International Organization for Migration and the human rights group the Walk Free Foundation, revealed that 28 million people are in forced labor and another 22 million in forced marriage.

Forced labor includes exploitation in domestic work, agriculture and manufacturing. It also includes state-imposed forced labor and commercial sexual exploitation. Poverty is a powerful driver for forced labor around the globe, particularly in India, East Asia and West Africa.

Forced marriage, mainly affecting women and girls, often has gendered, patriarchal roots.

The U.N.'s latest estimate of 50 million has grown substantially since its last estimate in 2017, when it reported 40 million persons were enslaved.

As someone who studies modern slavery, I am intrigued by global estimates.

Are there really 50 million persons living in slavery today as the U.N. claims?

What explains how the global estimate increased by 10 million over five years? Does that mean we will see an annual increase of 2 million slaves each year moving forward?

Getting Better at Global Estimates

Global estimates of modern slavery have improved over time.

In 2013, Walk Free's first Global Slavery Index reported 29.8 million persons enslaved.

But that estimate was based almost entirely on expert input instead of nationally representative random sample surveys – the gold standard of research design.

For its 2016 Global Slavery Index, Walk Free partnered with Gallup and commissioned random sample surveys for 25 countries.

By partnering with the world's premier polling organization and using advanced survey techniques, Walk Free was able to embark on groundbreaking work.

However, Walk Free ended up generating a global estimate for 168 nations, not just the 25 nations it had surveyed. That meant for the other countries in its 2016 estimate, Walk Free relied on both expert input and statistical techniques – and didn't solely use nationally representative survey data.

The Devil in the Details

That same technique of mixing survey data with statistical techniques applies to the U.N.'s 2017 and 2022 global estimates.

For its 2017 estimate, the U.N., working with Walk Free and other organizations, commissioned surveys in 48 countries from 2014 to 2016. And for its 2022 report, the U.N. gathered data from 68 countries to estimate forced marriage and from 75 countries to estimate forced labor.

Though the report revealed a clear increase in the number of nationally representative surveys to generate these global estimates, it still fell short in measuring a majority of the countries in the world.

There are currently 193 member states in the United Nations. The U.N.'s 2022 global estimate that surveyed 75 countries to estimate forced labor did not survey the remaining 118 countries, instead basing its numbers on expert input and statistical techniques.

Nor did the U.N. publish a full list of the countries for which it conducted nationally representative surveys in 2017. It's difficult, then, to know how many of those 48 countries sampled for the 2017 report were repeated for the 2022 report.

We also don't have publicly available data for those 48 countries, let alone the countries surveyed for the 2022 global estimate.

And without access to any of the statistical calculations made by the U.N. for either estimates, scholars cannot independently replicate the findings of the U.N. for either of its 2017 or 2022 reports.

Comparing Apples and Oranges

This lack of transparency makes it difficult to claim that there really was an increase of 10 million in the number of enslaved persons from 2017 to 2022.

Two things are happening here. The U.N. seems to be getting much better at estimating global slavery. But because the survey techniques are improving over time, it is impossible to make comparisons.

Consider the analogy of a bathroom scale. In weighing yourself, you might purchase an inexpensive scale at first just to get a rough idea of how much you weigh. But then, becoming more concerned about your health, you then purchase a much better scale that gives you a far more precise measurement.

This doesn't mean that your weight changed radically. It just means you now have a much better sense of your weight.

This analogy applies to measuring contemporary slavery.

The scale used by Walk Free was novel in 2013, and improved by 2016. The scale the U.N. used in 2017 was more precise, and the figures for 2022 got even better.

But to go back and say there are 10 million more persons enslaved today than there were in 2017 is not warranted.

Finding Clarity

Global estimates of modern slavery are eye-catching and important.

The 50 million figure today is one of the best estimates of modern slavery available and can prompt policymakers to take action. Without awareness of this crime, the problem cannot be solved.

Yet, moving forward, the public still needs more reliable, more valid and more transparent data. Science advances on the promise that data is freely available to enable others to replicate or improve the analysis.

Viewpoint 4

> *"Victims of trafficking are often placed in unsafe or illegal living or working conditions. Far from home, traffickers or employers force women and children into prostitution, sweatshop labor or other illegal activities."*

Precautions Can Help Prevent Human Trafficking

U.S. State Department

In the following viewpoint, the U.S. State Department defines what human trafficking is and what traffickers do to trick or coerce people into becoming trafficking victims. The State Department outlines specific techniques to protect oneself against becoming an unknowing victim of trafficking. The State Department maintains that there are many things one can do if they are seeking employment in the United States to prevent becoming trafficked. Although time has passed since this viewpoint was originally published, many of the tips and facts about human trafficking continue to apply today. The U.S. State Department is a department of the U.S. government that actively promotes the security and prosperity of the United States and its citizens.

"Be Smart, Be Safe," US Department of State, January 1, 2001.

As you read, consider the following questions:

1. According to the State Department, what types of jobs often serve as portals into human trafficking?
2. Can a person be forced to work in the U.S., as stated by the viewpoint?
3. According to this viewpoint, what happens to convicted traffickers in the U.S.?

What Is Trafficking?

Trafficking is when someone moves you from one place to another with the promise of giving you a job or offering you marriage by using coercion, fraud, deception and force. It is modern-day slavery and traffickers will not hesitate to harm you and your family.

Who Are the Victims of Trafficking?

Trafficking is a worldwide problem.

You may think "This cannot happen to me..." but it happens to people just like you all over the world every day. We do not want to scare you, but we want you to be safe.

Young women and children may be trafficked worldwide, into neighboring countries, or within their home countries.

Have you had an interesting offer to work abroad?

Every situation is different. You may or may not know that you are being trafficked and what you will be doing once you reach your destination.

> The woman suggested that she could help me to get work somewhere abroad. She told me she had an acquaintance in Germany, a woman who could connect me with a family for whom I could be a housemaid." Upon arrival... "She said I owed her 2,000 German marks and said that I would earn that money by providing sexual services to men. I was shocked!
>
> – Marsha, a trafficking survivor

Often women will answer newspaper advertisements for jobs without knowing that criminals are posing as legitimate businesses such as:

- Model agencies
- Travel agencies
- Employment companies
- "Au Pair" babysitting services
- International matchmaking services (mail order bride services)

These are only a few examples of the types of false businesses used by criminals.

> He told me then that I had been sold to him for $10,000, and that I would have to pay him back. He told me I would have to prostitute myself.
>
> – Olga, a trafficking survivor

However, traffickers are not always strangers, oftentimes women and children are "trafficked" by someone they know:

- A relative
- A neighbor
- An acquaintance/friend

Traffickers, who may be either criminal groups or individuals, will promise employment or marriage and will offer to handle and pay for the costs of a passport, work permit, and transportation for these women and children.

What Happens Next?

Victims of trafficking are often placed in unsafe or illegal living or working conditions. Far from home, traffickers or employers force women and children into prostitution, sweatshop labor or other illegal activities by:

- taking away documents: passports, birth certificates, identification cards, address books.

- debt bondage: once a person has signed a contract and reached their destination, the employer or individual will keep the person's salary to pay for the costs of travel, such as transportation, and passport and visa fees.
- physical abuse: punching, slapping, choking, pulling hair, kicking, forcing sex, and using a dangerous weapon such as a gun or knife.
- emotional and psychological abuse: threatening to hurt the family or take children away, threatening to turn the person over to police or immigration officers, destroying the person's property, humiliating and demeaning the person, forcing the person to commit illegal acts.
- isolation: being kept in a room or house with no contact with friends or social or religious groups.

> They beat me, but only across the back near the kidneys, so it would not hurt my appearance.
>
> – Olga

While some women know before they go that they will be exotic dancers, domestic workers, farm workers or prostitutes, they may find when they arrive they will also suffer isolation and abuse, and be forced to hand over most, if not all, of their earnings to their employers or sponsors.

How Can I Protect Myself?

If an individual or company is making plans for you to travel and work away from home:

- Know the address and telephone number of your country's embassy or consulate closest to where you will be staying.
- Learn the name, address and telephone number of where you are going. If possible, call or write to that employer to verify that you will be working there, and ask about your work, pay and living conditions.

- Check with a non-governmental organization (especially those who specialize in women's issues) in your country to help you determine if the person or company is legitimate or trustworthy; or, if you are traveling to the USA, contact the consular office at the United States Embassy.

Most legitimate employers will provide a contract. Do not sign any contracts right away. Read through the document. If there is something you do not understand, take the contract to an attorney, non-governmental organization, or someone you trust. Watch out for language that says the employer will:

- "hold all money in trust until your contract is completed";
- "subtract your cash allowance from the sum held in trust"; or
- "retain a percentage of your money."

Be suspicious if your prospective employer obtains a tourist visa for you to work in the U.S. (see U.S. laws below).

Tell your family and friends when you are leaving and give them the address where you will be staying.

When you arrive at your destination:

- Do not give your passport to anyone to keep for you! Regardless of your legal status, your employer does not need your passport and has no right to hold it.
- Keep a copy of your passport information in a safe place where only you can find it.
- Learn basic survival phrases in the local language.
- If you are in a foreign country, register with the embassy or consulate of your home country.
- Contact a family member or friend at home once you have reached your destination. Keep in contact with that person!

What Should I Know About the United States of America (U.S.A.)?

If I need help?

No one can force you to work in the United States!

Persons in the U.S. are protected by and subject to U.S. laws. Call the police if you are in danger or are being hurt. You have the right to be protected.

You have the right to a lawyer if you are arrested. If you do not have enough money for a lawyer, contact the local legal aid agency. You also have the right to speak to your embassy or consulate. If you are a victim of domestic violence, you can also get a protection order from the U.S. court that prohibits the abuser from attacking you or contacting you and your family.

A victim of crime in the U.S. has rights! Victim assistance programs provide many services such as counseling, emergency shelter, legal aid and emergency transportation.

- Call the Worker Exploitation Complaint Line: 1-888-428-7581. Translation is available for most non-English speakers.
- The complaint line receives calls about foreign workers who have been recruited or smuggled into the U.S. and are then forced to work under terrible conditions.
- The complaint line provides a referral service for exploited workers or victims of trafficking in need of medical and other basic services.
- This complaint line assists the U.S. government to prevent, investigate, and prosecute traffickers and persons who abuse workers in the United States.
- If you are in danger, dial 911, an emergency number that will get immediate help for you everywhere in the U.S.
- If you are afraid to go to the police, there are other places where you can get help:
    - Hospitals
    - Fire departments
    - Religious places
    - Shelters for women and children
    - Legal aid agencies
    - Immigrant services groups.

- Call your country's embassy or consulate in Washington, D.C. or a major U.S. city.

What Are the U.S. Laws?

Traffickers face up to 20 years or, under certain circumstances up to life in prison for each act of trafficking. Traffickers will also be forced to re-pay what they stole from the victim.

For traffickers: It is a crime to bring, or attempt to bring, someone into the U.S. at a place other than the port of entry, and to encourage or induce someone to come to, enter, or remain in the U.S. in violation of the law. It is a crime to harbor, conceal, or shield illegal foreigners from detection. Involuntary servitude and slavery are extremely serious crimes under U.S. law.

For illegal entry: It is a crime to enter the U.S. without being inspected by a U.S. immigration officer. The penalty is up to two years in prison and deportation. The U.S. Immigration and Naturalization Service (INS) can deport any person if they are in the U.S. illegally or are involved in illegal activities and deny them re-entry into the U.S.

For illegal work: It is illegal to work in the U.S. unless you have a visa which allows you to work, or the INS has formally authorized the work. To get work visas, you are required to appear personally for an interview before a U.S. Consular Officer (or an INS official if you are visiting the U.S. but want to work). Employment visas are reserved mostly for skilled laborers rather than jobs for waitressing and child care, or dancing in nightclubs. If you have questions about the requirements for a work visa, contact the nearest U.S. embassy or consulate.

For prostitution: Prostitution is illegal in nearly all cities and towns in the U.S. In addition, it is a crime to transport a person or promote his or her use as a prostitute. Transporting a person into the U.S., or across state borders within the U.S., with the purpose of having that person perform as a prostitute or for other illegal purposes is also a crime.

VIEWPOINT

> *"When a wealthy, powerful individual is implicated in sex trafficking, Americans seem to have a hard time holding the accused perpetrator accountable."*

Wealth and Privilege Protect Sex Traffickers

Bryan F. Alystock, Justin G. Witkin, Douglass A. Kreis, and Neil D. Overholtz

In the following viewpoint, lawyers from the law firm of Aylstock, Witkin, Kreis & Overholtz argue that rich and powerful individuals in America may not be held accountable for their crimes of sex trafficking as often as other people seen as typical criminals. The lawyers draw on the case of convicted sexual predator Jeffrey Epstein. The lawyers contend that Epstein received a lenient sentence and plea deal for his crimes because of his wealth and power. The viewpoint analyzes the way society and culture have conspired against women when it comes to sexual crimes including sex trafficking. The lawyers Bryan F. Alystock, Justin G. Witkin, Douglass A. Kreis, and Neil D. Overholtz are partners of a law firm based in Florida.

As you read, consider the following questions:

1. According to the authors, what protected Jeffrey Epstein from appropriate punishment?

"Sexual Predator Jeffrey Epstein and the Power of Privilege," Aylstock, Witkin, Kreis & Overholtz, PLLC, August 12, 2019. Reprinted by permission.

2. According to data cited in this viewpoint, what percent of sexual assault claims are false?
3. Why do women not report sexual crimes, according to this viewpoint?

Sex trafficking takes place in the seediest of motel rooms and in the most extravagant mansions of the rich and famous. Traffickers come from a diverse range of socioeconomic, racial and ethnic groups. Yet, when a wealthy, powerful individual is implicated in sex trafficking, Americans seem to have a hard time holding the accused perpetrator accountable. A recent case in point: millionaire financer Jeffrey Epstein.

In 2008, Epstein plead guilty to two counts of solicitation of prostitution; one of these charges involved soliciting a minor under the age of 18. Epstein served 13 months of an 18-month sentence in the private wing of the Palm Beach county jail. Anthony Acosta, appointed Labor Secretary by President Trump in 2017, was involved in Epstein's 2008 plea deal. In 2019, facing mounting criticism for facilitating such a lenient deal for the sex offender, Acosta resigned his position.

Epstein was arrested again in July of 2019 on charges of sex trafficking. Prosecutors accuse him of recruiting girls as young as 14 for sex at his New York and Palm Beach residences. According to federal law, any person under the age of 18 involved in a commercial sex act is a victim of sex trafficking. Epstein denied the trafficking charges. Epstein recently committed suicide while awaiting trial for these new trafficking charges, according to law enforcement sources.

Influential social connections and immense financial resources had allowed Jeffrey Epstein to assemble a team of powerful allies who protected him from being held accountable for his crimes. At least until recently. With the MeToo movement elevating the voices of sexual assault survivors, we are beginning to examine our assumptions about the kind of people we believe are – and are not – capable of sexual violence.

These kinds of conversations illuminate the dynamics of privilege. In an article for vox.com, Emily Crockett writes, "The idea that rape is a crime against a woman, and specifically a crime against a woman's body, is relatively new. For most of human history, rape has been treated as a property crime against a woman's husband or father, since they effectively owned her." While we may flatly reject the idea that women are the property of men, this mindset has deep roots that continue to penetrate our current thinking about sexual violence. Just listen to the interrogations that many survivors must contend with when their family, friends, law enforcement and the media learn about their assault: What were you wearing? Why were you walking there? Were you alone? Were you drinking? Did you flirt? It's as if we are saying: Your body is not your own. If you are not constantly vigilant, then of course somebody will take it.

After facing intense scrutiny of their appearance and motives, many sexual assault survivors find that their claims are simply dismissed. Implicitly or explicitly, they are told they are liars. Because of the trauma they endured, survivors may not be able to provide coherent, detailed narratives about the abuse. Crockett points out, "We are only just beginning to understand the science of how the brain processes trauma. Memories are stored in a fragmented way, and emotional reactions can seem 'off.' Both of these things can raise suspicions among police officers who are accustomed to using rigorous interrogations to ferret out inconsistencies in a story, and rigorous interrogation only makes things worse." According to the National Sexual Violence Resource Center, between 2 and 10 percent of sexual assaults are falsely reported. This means that the vast majority of sexual assault claims are true. Yet, despite these statistics, we continue to discount survivors. In an interview on PBS, writer and media critic Soraya Chemaly speaks about why many women do not disclose their abuse, "I think there's fear of shaming, of blaming, of retaliation, of being doubted. It's very hard, because we have a cultural predisposition to perpetuate a lot of rape myths. And one of those is that women excessively exaggerate as victims, that they make things up, that there are misinterpretations."

When we begin to deconstruct the entitlements that allow sexual perpetrators to continue to offend, we also expose the biases that silence and disempower their victims. These conversations begin to build a culture where even wealthy and powerful sexual predators like Jeffrey Epstein, as well as the allies and institutions that enable them, can finally be brought to justice. If you or someone you know is a survivor of sexual assault, please contact us to learn how our attorneys use civil law to hold perpetrators of sexual violence and the institutions who support them accountable.

Viewpoint 6

> *"In our recently published analysis, we found that contemporary slavery is a regular feature of armed conflict."*

War Drives Human Trafficking and Slavery

Monti Datta, Angharad Smith, and Kevin Bales

Although human trafficking and enslavement is a problem around the world, many cases take place in war-torn countries. The authors of this viewpoint used data from a leading database on war to examine how conflict intersects with human trafficking and modern slavery. Strategic enslavement can be used for tactical reasons or to promote genocide or ethnic cleansing. The governmental instability and poverty that often accompanies war only make these problems worse. Monti Datta is an associate professor of political science at the University of Richmond. Angharad Smith is the Modern Slavery Programme Officer at the Centre for Policy Research at United Nations University. Kevin Bales is a professor of contemporary slavery and research director of the Rights Lab at the University of Nottingham.

As you read, consider the following questions:

1. According to the authors' findings, how common is the use of slavery in modern armed conflicts?

"Slavery and war are tightly connected—but we had no idea just how much until we crunched the data," by Monti Datta, Angharad Smith, and Kevin Bales, The Conversation, August 22, 2022. https://theconversation.com/slavery-and-war-are-tightly-connected-but-we-had-no-idea-just-how-much-until-we-crunched-the-data-169904.

2. What database did the authors use to draw their conclusions?
3. What percentage of the cases of armed conflicts the authors studied included human trafficking?

Some 40 million people are enslaved around the world today, though estimates vary. Modern slavery takes many different forms, including child soldiers, sex trafficking and forced labor, and no country is immune. From cases of family controlled sex trafficking in the United States to the enslavement of fishermen in Southeast Asia's seafood industry and forced labor in the global electronics supply chain, enslavement knows no bounds.

As scholars of modern slavery, we seek to understand how and why human beings are still bought, owned and sold in the 21st century, in hopes of shaping policies to eradicate these crimes.

Many of the answers trace back to causes like poverty, corruption and inequality. But they also stem from something less discussed: war.

In 2016, the United Nations Security Council named modern slavery a serious concern in areas affected by armed conflict. But researchers still know little about the specifics of how slavery and war are intertwined.

We recently published research analyzing data on armed conflicts around the world to better understand this relationship.

What we found was staggering: The vast majority of armed conflict between 1989 and 2016 used some kind of slavery.

Coding Conflict

We used data from an established database about war, the Uppsala Conflict Data Program (UCDP), to look at how much, and in what ways, armed conflict intersects with different forms of contemporary slavery.

Our project was inspired by two leading scholars of sexual violence, Dara Kay Cohen and Ragnhild Nordås. These political scientists used that database to produce their own pioneering database about how rape is used as a weapon of war.

The Uppsala database breaks each conflict into two sides. Side A represents a nation state, and Side B is typically one or more nonstate actors, such as rebel groups or insurgents.

Using that data, our research team examined instances of different forms of slavery, including sex trafficking and forced marriage, child soldiers, forced labor and general human trafficking. This analysis included information from 171 different armed conflicts. Because the use of slavery changes over time, we broke multiyear conflicts into separate "conflict-years" to study them one year at a time, for a total of 1,113 separate cases.

Coding each case to determine what forms of slavery were used, if any, was a challenge. We compared information from a variety of sources, including human rights organizations like Amnesty International and Human Rights Watch, scholarly accounts, journalists' reporting and documents from governmental and intergovernmental organizations.

Alarming Numbers

In our recently published analysis, we found that contemporary slavery is a regular feature of armed conflict. Among the 1,113 cases we analyzed, 87% contained child soldiers – meaning fighters age 15 and younger – 34% included sexual exploitation and forced marriage, about 24% included forced labor and almost 17% included human trafficking.

A global heat map of the frequency of these armed conflicts over time paints a sobering picture. Most conflicts involving enslavement take place in low-income countries, often referred to as the Global South.

About 12% of the conflicts involving some form of enslavement took place in India, where there are several conflicts between the government and nonstate actors. Teen militants are involved in conflicts such as the insurgency in Kashmir and the separatist movement in Assam. About 8% of cases took place in Myanmar,

5% in Ethiopia, 5% in the Philippines and about 3% in Afghanistan, Sudan, Turkey, Colombia, Pakistan, Uganda, Algeria and Iraq.

This evidence of enslavement predominately in the Global South may not be surprising, given how poverty and inequality can fuel instability and conflict. However, it helps us reflect upon how these countries' historic, economic and geopolitical relationships to the Global North also fuel pressure and violence, a theme we hope slavery researchers can study in the future.

Strategic Enslavement

Typically, when armed conflict involves slavery, it's being used for tactical aims: building weapons, for example, or constructing roads and other infrastructure projects to fight a war. But sometimes, slavery is as part of an overarching strategy. In the Holocaust, the Nazis used "strategic slavery" in what they called "extermination through labor." Today, as in the past, strategic slavery is normally part of a larger strategy of genocide.

We found that "strategic enslavement" took place in about 17% of cases. In other words, enslavement was one of the primary objectives of about 17% of the conflicts we examined, and often served the goal of genocide. One example is the Islamic State's enslavement of the Yazidi minority in the 2014 massacre in Sinjar, Iraq. In addition to killing Yazidis, the Islamic State sought to enslave and impregnate women for systematic ethnic cleansing, attempting to eliminate the ethnic identity of the Yazidi through forced rape.

The connections between slavery and conflict are vicious but still not well understood. Our next steps include coding historic cases of slavery and conflict going back to World War II, such as how Nazi Germany used forced labor and how Imperial Japan's military used sexual enslavement. We have published a new data set, "Contemporary Slavery in Armed Conflict," and hope other researchers will also use it to help better understand and prevent future violence.

Viewpoint 7

> *"The crucial point of trafficking is the abuse of power to exploit another human being. It thrives in conditions of poverty, economic and gender inequality, corruption and instability."*

There Are Many Common Misconceptions About How Child Trafficking Happens

Alexandra Baxter

This viewpoint by Alexandra Baxter argues that although stereotypes and conspiracy theories lead many people to believe that most child victims of human trafficking are kidnapped by strangers and forced into sex trafficking, the data does not back this up. In reality, child abduction and cases of sexual abuse by strangers are relatively rare in the United States, as American children are much more likely to be abused by an adult they know and trust. There are millions of victims of sex slavery and trafficking, but most come from countries where poverty and economic and social vulnerability are rampant issues, though they are trafficked around the world. At the time this viewpoint was published, Alexandra Baxter was a PhD candidate in criminology/law at Flinders University in Australia.

"Want to save the children? How child sexual abuse and human trafficking really work," by Alexandra Baxter, The Conversation, May 10, 2021. https://theconversation.com/want-to-save-the-children-how-child-sexual-abuse-and-human-trafficking-really-work-153288.

As you read, consider the following questions:

1. According to data cited in this viewpoint, what is the most common scenario involving missing children?
2. According to the U.N.'s definition of human trafficking, does a person have to be moved from one place to another to be trafficked?
3. According to data cited in this viewpoint, what percent of trafficking victims are children under 18 who are trafficked for labor?

Millions of kidnapped children are imprisoned in underground tunnels, being sexually abused and tortured by a shadowy global cabal of paedophiles.

That, at least, is some of the misinformation about child sex trafficking being spread on social media. You'll also see such ideas being promoted at protests from Los Angeles to London, with hashtags such as #saveourchildren and #endchildtrafficking emblazoned on shirts and placards.

The thought of a child being abused, exploited or trafficked for sex elicits a powerful emotional response. These lurid tales have proven to be a potent gateway for mothers (and others) to "go down the rabbithole".

The tragedy is that misinformation is turning well-intentioned people into "digital soldiers" unwittingly working against genuine efforts to eliminate child sexual abuse and human trafficking.

Let's try to untangle the misconceptions.

The Truth About Child Sexual Abuse

Statistics on child sexual abuse are never exact. Less than 40% of victims report being abused when children. The average time before disclosure, according to Australia's Royal Commission into Institutional Responses to Child Sexual Abuse, is about 20 years for women and 25 years for men. Some never disclose.

There are enough robust studies, however, to suggest about one in ten children are sexually abused before age 18 – one in seven girls (14%) and one in 25 boys (4%).

Most typically the abuser is an adult known and trusted by the child and their parents. Then by a non-biological relative or in-law. In fewer than 15% of cases is the perpetrator a stranger.

A 2000 study for the US Bureau of Justice Statistics found 7.5% of all known female victims under the age of 17, and 5% of male victims, were abused by a stranger. More recent data published in 2016 by the Australian Bureau of Statistics found strangers accounted for 11.5% of sexual abuse of girls under the age of 16, and 15% of boys.

The differences between these findings are most likely due to greater awareness reducing opportunities for abuse by "acquaintances" such as clergy, teachers and coaches. In the 2000 data, to illustrate, 69% of molested boys were abused by an acquaintance; in the 2016 data it was about 47%.

Exaggerating Stranger Danger

Media coverage tends to distort understanding of child sexual abuse. It focuses on "stranger danger" and amplifies the threat of children being molested at the park or shopping centre.

Even more intense coverage goes to the rarer cases where children are abducted or murdered. Think of the fascination with cases such as the 2007 disappearance of three-year-old Madeleine McCann. But such cases are memorable because they are so rare.

The so-called "Pastel-Q" conspiracy theory, however, asserts millions of children a year are being kidnapped and trafficked for sex.

This claim rests on misrepresented numbers from missing persons reports. In the case of the US, for example, the claim is that 800,000 children disappear each year. (A similar rate applied globally would mean about 19 million children disappear every year.)

In fact, the FBI's data shows the number of people under the age of 17 reported missing in the US in 2020 was about 365,000. In most cases (based on several decades' of data) these missing reports involve a child running away from home or being taken by a custodial parent. Almost half are found within three hours, and more than 99% are found alive. Since 2010, in the US fewer than 350 people a year under the age of 21 have been abducted by strangers.

Sex Trafficking in Reality

So no, there's no evidence millions of children in wealthy nations are being kidnapped by paedophiles.

This is not to say child sex trafficking isn't a serious concern. But it is a different problem to the Pastel-Q portrayal.

The United Nations' Trafficking in Persons Protocol defines human trafficking as:

> the recruitment, transportation, transfer, harbouring or receipt of persons, by means of the threat or use of force or other forms of coercion, of abduction, of fraud, of deception, of the abuse of power or of a position of vulnerability or of the giving or receiving of payments or benefits to achieve the consent of a person having control over another person, for the purpose of exploitation

This means human trafficking doesn't necessarily require moving a person from one place to another, in the way we think of weapons and drugs being trafficked. It's not the same as people smuggling. Nor is it exactly the same as modern slavery, although there is broad crossover in definitions.

The crucial point of trafficking is the abuse of power to exploit another human being. It thrives in conditions of poverty, economic and gender inequality, corruption and instability. It requires systemic solutions, which the cartoonish constructions of Pastel-Q distract attention from.

Trafficking and Modern Slavery

Accurately estimating the true scale of child sex trafficking is, like child sexual abuse, complicated. There is the hidden nature of these crimes, differences in policing and reporting between nations, and little uniformity in how statistics are compiled.

The United Nations' Global Report on Trafficking in Persons only reports on "detected" cases. There are no more than 25,000 cases each year.

But researchers have good reasons to believe this is just the tip of the iceberg. The most commonly accepted estimates of the true number of trafficking victims in the world is about 21 million. About 16 million have been trafficked for labour; about 3 million of these are aged under 18.

About 5 million are trafficked for sex – most typically by being coerced into sex work. More than 99% of sex-trafficking victims are women. More than 70% are in Asia, followed by Europe and Central Asia (14%), Africa (8%), the Americas (4%), and the Arab States (1%). About a million are aged under 18.

We must be cautious about these total estimates. Nonetheless there is sufficient research to be confident only a very small percentage of cases involve scenarios like that in the movie *Taken*, where Liam Neeson's character uses his "very particular set of skills" to rescue his kidnapped 17-year-old American daughter from sex slavery.

More often, traffickers approach families living in poverty or socially and economically vulnerable girls – such as runaways – offering false promises of affection, work and a better life. Instead the girls find themselves being pressured or coerced into sex work.

This was the case with the victims of Jeffrey Epstein, whose intermediaries lured girls aged 14 to 18 with cash to perform massages, then nude massages, then sex.

How Do We Address This?

Child sexual abuse and child sex trafficking are both serious global problems. We should all be concerned about them.

But they can't be divorced from the broader conditions that allow many more millions of children and adults to be trafficked and exploited as modern slaves.

They require sophisticated, holistic and broad-based legal and policy responses. They will not be tackled by misunderstanding their reality and complexity, and indulging in false narratives that divert attention from the real issues.

Which is why more than 130 anti-trafficking organisations have said anybody who lends credibility to these false claims "actively harms the fight against human trafficking".

Periodical and Internet Sources Bibliography

The following articles have been selected to supplement the diverse views presented in this chapter.

Therese Apel, "Experts: Gangs Are Key in Human Trafficking Industry," WLBT, February 11, 2021. https://www.wlbt.com/2021/02/12/experts-gangs-are-key-human-trafficking-industry/.

Jaclyn Diaz, "The 1.5 Million Children Who Fled Ukraine Are at Risk of Human Trafficking," NPR, March 19, 2022. https://www.npr.org/2022/03/19/1087749861/ukraine-children-unicef-risk-report-human-trafficking.

Hannah Gould, "What Fuels Human Trafficking," UNICEF, January 13, 2017. https://www.unicefusa.org/stories/what-fuels-human-trafficking/31692.

Micah Hartmann, "Causes and Effects of Human Trafficking," the Exodus Road, July 6, 2021. https://theexodusroad.com/causes-effects-of-human-trafficking/.

Carl Hiaasen, "Jeffrey Epstein's Wealth, Power Gave Him Protection That His Victims Never Got," *TRIB Live*, October 12, 2022. https://triblive.com/opinion/carl-hiaasen-jeffrey-epsteins-wealth-power-gave-him-protection-that-his-victims-never-got/.

Amy Kerr, "Child Trafficking," Poverty Child, December 7, 2021. https://povertychild.org/child-trafficking/.

Tariro Mzezewa, "Homeless Youth at High Risk of Human Trafficking," *New York Times*, April 17, 2017. https://archive.nytimes.com/kristof.blogs.nytimes.com/2017/04/17/homeless-youth-at-high-risk-of-human-trafficking.

Katie Reilly, "How the #Me Too Movement Helped Make New Charges Against Jeffrey Epstein Possible," *TIME*, July 9, 2019. https://time.com/5621958/jeffrey-epstein-charges-me-too-movement/.

Jarrod Sadulski, "Gangs Have Set Their Sights on Human Trafficking Victims," American Military University/EDGE,

November 13, 2020. https://amuedge.com/gangs-have-set-their-sights-on-human-trafficking-victims/.

Daniele Selby, "Jeffrey Epstein Scandal: An Important Reminder Thousands of Girls Are Trafficked Across the US," Global Citizen, July 18, 2019. https://www.globalcitizen.org/en/content/jeffrey-epstein-sex-trafficking-us/.

Chapter 2

How Do Businesses Drive and Prevent Human Trafficking?

Chapter Preface

There is no question that a country cannot have a stable, functioning economy without a healthy financial system. Individuals, businesses, local governments, the federal government, and many more entities combine to make up a country's financial system. But what if that same system somehow—either knowingly or unknowingly—supports illegal activities? Is there anything the financial sector, individual businesses, and other profit-motivated industries can do to discourage human trafficking, and what do they do to encourage trafficking to begin with?

People everywhere must work in some way in order to earn money to support themselves and their families. Businesses and corporations must do the same thing to survive—they must make profits to sustain their operations. Unfortunately, this is no different whether the business is a legal or illegal enterprise. And human trafficking has proven to be a lucrative business both in the United States and around the world.

The viewpoints in this chapter illustrate how the financial system and businesses intersect with the practice of human trafficking. Jamille Bigio takes a look at the function of profitability in human trafficking, while Brian Monroe and the U.S. State Department provide details on how financial institutions can work to combat human trafficking. Ali Iqbal, Aliya Khan, and Susie Hughes examine how money from wealthy organ "transplant tourists" fuel a global organ trafficking system that exploits poor and persecuted members of society, demonstrating how profit drives trafficking in other sectors as well.

Not surprisingly, monetary and financial gain play a major role in human trafficking. The viewpoints in this chapter examine the role that finance and other industries play.

Viewpoint 1

> *"Human trafficking bankrolls operations for transnational crime syndicates and extremist groups; forced labor produces an estimated $150 billion annually for perpetrators, making it one of the world's most profitable crimes."*

Human Trafficking Is Extremely Profitable

Jamille Bigio

In the following viewpoint Jamille Bigio demonstrates that one of the bottom-line difficulties in combating human trafficking is the money it brings in. Bigio outlines multiple instances that demonstrate the tenacity of trafficking around the world due to the fact that it is a highly profitable enterprise used by groups and individuals in many countries. Bigio contends that although the U.S. government and public maintains that it wants to prevent trafficking, some behaviors suggest otherwise. Jamille Bigio is a former director for human rights and gender on the White House National Security Council staff.

As you read, consider the following questions:

1. According to Bigio, what are two countries that use trafficking for financial gains?

"Human Trafficking Helps Terrorists Earn Money and Strategic Advantage," by Jamille Bigio, Foreign Policy, January 31, 2020. Reprinted by permission.

2. What are two specific monetary ways that trafficking is beneficial for traffickers, as reported by the author?
3. How have American companies profited from trafficking, as stated in the viewpoint?

Twenty years ago, global leaders from nearly 120 countries joined forces through a new U.N. convention to agree on a universal definition of human trafficking and recommit themselves to ridding the world of it. That same year, the U.S. government enacted the Trafficking Victims Protection Act to close gaps in U.S. law. Yet, despite near-universal pledges to eradicate the crime, human trafficking and modern slavery continue unabated, affecting more than 40 million people worldwide.

This failure poses a global threat: While human trafficking is rightfully condemned as a grave affront to human rights and dignity, it persists unchecked. As the United States renews its commitment to protecting freedom and ending slavery—with its annual observation of National Slavery and Human Trafficking Prevention this month, culminating on National Freedom Day on Feb. 1—it should address the many ways that human trafficking imperils global security. Indeed, this practice supports terrorist and armed groups, bankrolls criminal organizations, enables abusive regimes, and undermines stability, according to a recent Council on Foreign Relations report written with my colleague, Rachel Vogelstein.

Part of the problem is that armed and violent extremist groups use trafficking as a direct tactic of war, generating profits and advancing their strategic aims. Insurgent groups—from central Africa's Lord's Resistance Army to Libyan militias—have used captives to expand military capabilities and support operations, with victims forced to serve as combatants, messengers, cooks, porters, and spies. Other terrorist organizations—including the Islamic State and Boko Haram—engage in sex trafficking. They use enslaved women to attract and mobilize male fighters and generate significant revenue as well. In 2014 alone, ransom payments extracted by the Islamic State amounted to between $35 million and $45 million. In other words, such groups use trafficking to expand their power and capabilities, thereby prolonging conflict.

The scale of the problem is only growing, exacerbated by global challenges including forced migration. Refugees and migrants are at particularly high risk of both labor and sex trafficking, and their numbers are increasing—by the end of 2018, more than 70 million people had been forcibly displaced by violence, conflict, and persecution, close to double the figure a decade ago. Their lack of legal status leaves refugees and migrants vulnerable to exploitation; traffickers deliberately deceive workers about their country of final destination and their living and working conditions.

Transnational criminal groups in Southeast Asia, for example, prey on Rohingya refugees fleeing persecution in Myanmar, promising them lucrative employment in Malaysia only to hold them captive at sea in fishing vessels or in trafficking camps along the Malaysia-Thailand border. Traffickers earn an estimated $60,000 per ship by selling victims into further exploitation or demanding ransom from captives' families, generating between $50 million and $100 million annually. In Central America, smugglers, criminals, and traffickers—emboldened by restrictive and punitive U.S. immigration policies—capitalize on migrants' desperation to reach safety in the United States: Smugglers charge migrants exorbitant fees, and some leverage debt into forced labor or sexual exploitation. In that way, human trafficking bankrolls operations for transnational crime syndicates and extremist groups; forced labor produces an estimated $150 billion annually for perpetrators, making it one of the world's most profitable crimes.

Beyond emboldening terrorist groups and bankrolling criminal activity, human trafficking also supports abusive regimes. Some repressive governments traffic their own citizens and compel them to labor in harsh conditions in order to bolster the economy or suppress dissent. The U.S. State Department estimates that the North Korean government, for example, has close to 100,000 forced laborers working abroad, mainly in China and Russia, often in harsh conditions. By taxing those overseas workers, the regime has generated more than $500 million annually, thereby helping it mitigate the effects of economic sanctions.

Even peacekeeping missions and military installations have contributed to an increase in human trafficking from the Balkans to Haiti to South Korea. Between 2001 and 2011, one study found that the presence of peacekeeping forces was positively correlated with forced prostitution, damaging public perceptions of the United Nations. Last year, U.S. government inspectors uncovered abuses by Defense Department contractors participating in labor trafficking. The contractors were allegedly hiring workers from third-party countries to work in a variety of support jobs—including food services—on U.S. bases in Kuwait (an issue previously documented on U.S. bases in Iraq); investigators found that the contractors had illegally charged recruitment fees to the victims, housed them in substandard conditions, and withheld their passports. Perpetrating sex and labor trafficking diminishes U.S. influence in tackling the very same crime.

The human cost that trafficking exacts on communities is detrimental and long lasting: the associated stigma—particularly in instances of sexual exploitation and children being used by armed groups—marginalizes survivors, creating a cycle of poverty that is difficult to break and impeding the recovery efforts in post-conflict societies

Despite the security implications of human trafficking, convictions for trafficking offenses are rare, programs focused on prevention and protection are underresourced, and most efforts to address human trafficking are detached from broader conflict prevention, security, and counterterrorism initiatives. The issue of trafficking has been seen as a concern primarily of human rights activists, not of the national security community. However, a growing body of research and evidence suggests that as security threats converge, human trafficking becomes a threat multiplier, since it finances other criminal activities and foments greater insecurity.

Viewpoint 

> *"Transplant operations in China increased rapidly in the early 2000s without a corresponding rise in voluntary organ donors, which led to questions about the source of the organs."*

Organ Transplantation in North America Drives Organ Trafficking

Ali Iqbal, Aliya Khan, and Susie Hughes

Millions of patients around the world depend on organ transplantation to save their lives, but this viewpoint explains the dark side of organ transplant programs. The authors explain that the organ trafficking industry exploits poor and persecuted members of society to benefit wealthy transplant tourists, many of whom are from North America. In particular, this viewpoint examines the practice of forced organ harvesting in China, in which prisoners are executed so their organs can be harvested and "donated" to patients in need of organ transplants. Ali Iqbal is a transplant nephrologist and assistant professor of medicine at McMaster University, where Aliya Khan is a clinical professor on the faculty of health sciences. Susie Hughes is executive director of End Transplant Abuse in China.

"Killing prisoners for transplants: Forced organ harvesting in China," by Ali Iqbal, Aliya Khan, and Susie Hughes, The Conversation, July 28, 2022. https://theconversation.com/killing-prisoners-for-transplants-forced-organ-harvesting-in-china-161999.

As you read, consider the following questions:

1. How does China's transplant program rank globally?
2. When did transplant operations start to increase in China?
3. What raised concerns about the issue of forced organ harvesting?

Organ transplantation is a life-saving therapy for millions of patients and one of the greatest successes of modern medicine. However, a limited supply of donor organs, paired with a massive demand for transplants, has fuelled the global organ trafficking industry which exploits poor, underprivileged and persecuted members of society as a source of organs to be purchased by wealthy transplant tourists.

Although this practice occurs in many countries, the situation in China is particularly concerning. China is the only country in the world to have an industrial-scale organ trafficking practice that harvests organs from executed prisoners of conscience. This practice is known as forced organ harvesting.

To understand forced organ harvesting, it is useful to consider a hypothetical scenario: a patient in Canada with end-stage heart disease is in need of a life-saving cardiac transplant.

Doctors in Canada tell the patient he needs to go on a waiting list until a compatible donor dies under suitable conditions. This process can take weeks, months or even years. The patient then finds a transplant program in China that can schedule a cardiac transplant from a compatible donor weeks in advance.

This raises several important questions. Cardiac transplant can only come from deceased donors, so how can the hospital match this patient with a potential "deceased" donor weeks in advance? How did the hospital find this donor? How do they know when that donor will die? Has the donor consented to have their organs harvested?

Distressing Facts

The answers to these questions are extremely distressing. China uses incarcerated prisoners of conscience as an organ donor pool to provide compatible transplants for patients. These prisoners or "donors" are executed and their organs harvested against their will, and used in a prolific and profitable transplant industry.

As transplant nephrologists and medical professionals, we aim to spread awareness about organ trafficking, particularly forced organ harvesting, to colleagues, institutions, patients and the public. We are involved with organizations like Doctors Against Forced Organ Harvesting and International Coalition to End Transplant Abuse in China, which have done considerable work in this area for over a decade.

China currently has the second-largest transplant program in the world. Transplant operations in China increased rapidly in the early 2000s without a corresponding rise in voluntary organ donors, which led to questions about the source of the organs.

During this period of rapid transplant growth, practitioners of the Buddhist Qi gong discipline known as Falun Gong, were being detained, persecuted and killed in large numbers by the Chinese government. Similarly, China in 2017 began a campaign of mass detention, surveillance, sterilization and forced labour against the Uyghur ethnic group of Xinjiang.

Human Rights Investigations

Concerns about forced organ harvesting began to surface in 2006-7 by the work of two international human rights lawyers, David Kilgour and David Matas, who were later nominated for a Nobel Peace Prize for their work. The China Tribunal, led by human rights lawyer Sir Geoffrey Nice, was formed in 2019 to independently investigate the claims of forced organ harvesting.

The Tribunal examined multiple lines of evidence, including transplant numbers, medical testing of detained prisoners, recorded phone calls to transplant hospitals, as well as testimony from surgeons and prisoners. The final conclusion was issued in March of 2020 and "confirmed beyond reasonable doubt" that China had been using executed prisoners of conscience as a source of transplant organs for many years.

Despite Chinese transplant officials claiming significant transplant reform had taken place since 2015, recent evidence suggests that the barbaric practice of forced organ harvesting has continued. The *American Journal of Transplantation*, the world's leading transplant journal, published a paper in April that found that brain death had not been declared in many organ retrievals in China, and that retrieval of the donor's vital organs was the actual cause of death. In other words, these prisoners were being executed by removal of their organs for the purpose of transplantation.

The International Society of Heart and Lung Transplantation issued a policy statement in June that excludes submissions that are "related to transplantation and involving either organs or tissue from human donors in the People's Republic of China."

Raising Awareness

Unfortunately, the use of unethical medical practices against marginalized groups is not new. The Nazis conducted horrific experiments on Jewish victims in concentration camps. Soviet psychiatrists created a term known as sluggish schizophrenia to label political dissidents, depriving them of civic rights, employment and credibility. American researchers studied the effects of untreated syphilis in African Americans in the Tuskegee study.

China has been executing prisoners of conscience and using their organs for transplantation for decades. Transplant physicians, medical professionals and the global community must raise awareness and pressure governments, institutions and hospitals to take action.

It is essential that we conduct due diligence and avoid collaborations where transparency regarding the source of organs cannot be guaranteed. We must protest the unjust and inhumane incarceration and oppression of Uyghurs and marginalized groups around the world.

We must encourage organ donor registration and support initiatives that increase donation to ultimately curb the demand for illegal organ trafficking.

Viewpoint 3

> *"Like banks, crypto exchanges need to better understand how human trafficking can occur through their platforms."*

Ways for Banks to Stop Human Trafficking During Transactions

Brian Monroe

In the following viewpoint, Brian Monroe argues that financial systems, banks, and cryptocurrency exchanges are uniquely situated to help identify the issue of human trafficking, and consequently to help prevent it. Monroe identifies the problem and explains that the market of human trafficking is exploding because it is financially lucrative. He outlines and explains clues that financial service providers can use to spot human trafficking groups using their services to unload money. Brian Monroe is a journalist and writer in the field of financial crimes.

As you read, consider the following questions:

1. As explained throughout the viewpoint, what are suspicious activity reports?
2. According to the author, what are two red flags in the financial system that could indicate suspicious behavior?

"Top Five Ways to Detect, Counter Human Trafficking in Bank, Crypto Exchange Transactions," by Brian Monroe, CFCS, January 30, 2020. Reprinted by permission. https://www.acfcs.org/top-five-ways-to-detect-counter-human-trafficking-in-bank-crypto-exchange-transactions/

3. As stated in this viewpoint, which systems make it easier to spot suspicious financial behavior?

The scourge of human trafficking is one of the fastest growing crimes in the world today, generating billions of dollars in profits annually for a wide range of illicit operations, from large organized criminal groups to low-level opportunists who are adept at taking advantage of the vulnerable and desperate.

Not surprisingly, as financial institutions better train their counter-crime teams to identify the red flags of potential human trafficking, criminals are making it harder for anti-money laundering (AML) officers to uncover and law enforcement to investigate their networks by flowing illicit funds into the virtual world by using crypto coins and related exchanges.

Like banks, crypto exchanges need to better understand how human trafficking can occur through their platforms and boost the number of suspicious activity reports (SARs) operations are filing, a duty only magnified with January being National Slavery and Human Trafficking Prevention Month.

At least for the brick-and-mortar brethren of the crypto sector, trafficking SARs have soared in the last year.

For example, the number or SARs tied to human trafficking filed by banks and money services exploded from 109 in 2018 to 3,384 in 2019, chiefly due a recently-added checkbox for the crime and last year being the first full year of reporting, according to the U.S. Treasury's Financial Crimes Enforcement Network (FinCEN) and analysis by Dynamic Securities Analytics.

Banks accounted for 70 percent of the human trafficking SAR filings. As well, banks reported US Currency as the instrument used in 45 percent of Human Trafficking SARs. Banks also reported Funds Transfers in 34 percent and checks 13 percent of human trafficking SARs.

It's critical that crypto exchanges also take an informed and proactive stance against trafficking through their operations because the crime is rising dramatically.

In recent years, the "number of victims of human trafficking and migrant smuggling has continued to grow significantly," according to a 2018 report by the Paris-based Financial Action Task Force (FATF), noting that revenues have more than quadrupled in less than a decade—the last time the watchdog group gauged the pulse of the sector and released guidance.

In addition to the "terrible human cost," the estimated proceeds that human trafficking generates have increased from $32 billion to more than $150 billion since FATF produced a comprehensive report on the laundering of the proceeds of these crimes in 2011.

At the same time, there is also a "better understanding of how and where human trafficking is taking place, including the increasing prevalence of people being trafficked in the same country or region," according to the FATF report, noting that such details can give additional color and context to simply viewing aberrant financials alone.

But those massive financial figures also open the door to getting on the radar of law enforcement and being uncovered by financial crime compliance professionals.

Overall, the financial industry—when properly trained, tuned and sensitized to the human and transactional tells of human trafficking—is in a unique position to combat this heinous crime, with banks, money services businesses and other operations subject to AML rules more aggressively identifying and reporting on such crimes in recent years.

In conjunction with the Anti-Human Trafficking Intelligence Initiative (ATII), a newly-formed non-profit devoted to sharing knowledge on trafficking typologies, building counter-trafficking data sets and supporting victims, ACFCS is offering some of the top tips to help professionals better uncover potential instances of trafficking when it intersects the crypto world.

"We want to get cryptocurrency exchanges to practice corporate social responsibility, consider implementing anti-human trafficking training, data, best practices and make a stand as an organization when considering working with customers utilizing unsavory systems, sites and practicing illicit activities," said Aaron Kahler, ATII's Founder and Chief Executive.

"These exchanges also should consider the negative impact their organizations can incur as investigations into human trafficking, child exploitation and other criminal activities ramp up within the crypto space," he said, noting that crypto exchanges with strong AML programs can be part of the solution, not the problem.

That was borne out in the "Welcome-to-video" investigation, where crypto exchanges with strong AML programs were critical in helping law enforcement take down the dark web child sexual exploitation video site that attempted to use digital value to anonymize users.

Human Trafficking Crypto-Related Red Flags

Small transactions, big clues: Frequent purchases in multiples of small amounts of Bitcoin or virtual currencies, directly by the client or through exchanges.

How Financial Services Fight Human Trafficking

As the second largest illicit business in the world (after drug trafficking), human trafficking yields an estimated $150 billion in illicit profits each year. This is a result of criminal enslavement and exploitation of approximately 21 million people worldwide. It is also among the world's most under-reported crimes.

Given the scale and pervasiveness of human trafficking, businesses can inadvertently expose their business to risk unless they seek to identify and tackle the issue in their supply chain. In an effort to combat this crime, financial institutions are increasingly going beyond their standard anti-money laundering protocols to flush out human trafficking activity - other industries could learn from this too.

"Financial Services Helping Tackle Human Trafficking," Grant Thornton, May 9, 2017.

On the prowl for night owls: Engaging in crypto transactions between 11 p.m. and 5 a.m., particularly on weekends. This is also a classic red flag for operations like massage parlors that they may be up to no good with trafficked labor.

Properly classifying the classifieds: Engaging in crypto transactions—either directly or tied to prepaid and credit cards—to make large/frequent purchases related to food, motel/hotel rooms, movies and entertainment, vehicle rentals, phones, advertisements and online classified websites.

It's personal this time: Using Bitcoin or other virtual currencies to make payments to sites associated with the adult industry or offering escort, massage and related "personal" services.

Be awoken with tokens: Using virtual currencies to purchase tokens associated with or specifically designed for the adult industry.

Adult Sites Taking Crypto Deposits in the 'SpankBank'

Some adult sites are already creating tokenized systems mirroring certain crypto platforms in a bid to make it harder for institutions to see the whole transaction picture and uncover possible instances of human trafficking.

"Attribution is key in order to detect Human Trafficking activity with Crypto Currency," said Larry Cameron, the Chief Information Security Officer at ATII. "We are all familiar with BackPage but there are other tokens, products and ecosystems that are designed specifically for the Adult Industry."

For example, he noted that a new adult-themed, Ethereum-based digital value system, SPANK, has emerged in recent months, offering conversion from and to fiat currencies and BOOTY tokens, which, appropriately enough, you can also hold in a SpankBank on the SpankChain Network.

Such a system "goes beyond and attempts to undermine laws and traditional banking by providing payment systems for the Adult Industry," Cameron said, noting that SPANK advertises products like Booty Token, SpankBank, SpankPay and CryptoT-tties, which would ostensibly allow users to pay for adult services with less law enforcement interference and without as many transactional tells being seen by bank and credit card monitoring systems.

"These systems are designed for exploitation, but they also make it easier to detect and trace the funds" he said. "When these sites are properly attributed and cataloged it makes it easy to detect Human Trafficking activity."

Viewpoint 4

> *"One of the most effective ways to identify broader criminal networks and take the profit out of this crime is to follow the financial trail human traffickers leave behind."*

The Financial Sector Can Help Eradicate the Profit of Human Trafficking

U.S. State Department

In the following viewpoint, the U.S. State Department maintains that financial institutions are a vital ally in the deterrence of human trafficking. The State Department argues that with proper training, financial officers can help spot illegal activity. By law, banks and other institutions in the financial sector are required to report suspicious behavior to the proper authorities. The State Department points out that technology is used by traffickers, but technology can also be used to stop trafficking, and to help victims. The U.S. State Department is a department of the U.S. government that actively promotes the security and prosperity of the United States and its citizens.

As you read, consider the following questions:

1. What is one of the best ways that the financial sector can help deter trafficking, as reported in the viewpoint?

"The Role of the Financial Sector: Promising Practices in the Eradication of Trafficking in Persons," US Department of State, July 1, 2021.

2. Which U.S. law mandates that financial institutions monitor and report suspicious activities, according to the author?
3. According to this viewpoint, which types of technology do human traffickers typically use?

Human trafficking is a widespread and highly profitable crime that generates an estimated $150 billion worldwide per year with a significant portion of those profits passing through legitimate financial services businesses. The illicit financial activity that human trafficking generates includes, but is not limited to: payments associated with the transport of victims and other logistics such as hotels or plane tickets; collection of proceeds generated by the exploitation of trafficking victims and by the sale of goods produced through their exploitation; movement of proceeds; and bribery and corrupt dealings to facilitate human trafficking.

One of the most effective ways to identify broader criminal networks and take the profit out of this crime is to follow the financial trail human traffickers leave behind. With proper training and guidance, financial institutions and designated non-financial businesses are able to identify illicit finance related to human trafficking and report potential cases. In addition, legal experts state that taking a "financial crimes approach" to human trafficking is highly effective in generating financial evidence that allows law enforcement to differentiate the traffickers from their victims, document the traffickers' motives and knowledge, corroborate victim testimony, and assist in identifying affiliates. Proactive partnerships between governments, financial institutions, law enforcement, civil society, and survivor experts are critical to identifying illicit financial activity associated with human trafficking. Removing the ability to profit from the crime disincentivizes traffickers and serves as a crucial deterrent to prevent the crime altogether.

The Role of Governments and the Financial Sector

The UN TIP Protocol, which is widely ratified, mandates the criminalization of money laundering when proceeds are derived from human trafficking and encourages signatories to promote international cooperation between their respective national authorities addressing money laundering. The Financial Action Task Force (FATF) is the global standard-setting body for anti-money laundering (AML), countering the financing of terrorism, and countering proliferation financing. More than 200 countries have agreed to implement the FATF Recommendations, which require member countries to identify, assess, and understand money laundering and illicit finance risks and to mitigate those risks. The FATF Recommendations provide a useful framework for jurisdictions to address illicit finance related to human trafficking by strengthening their national AML laws and policies and by improving coordination and information sharing domestically and internationally. The FATF Recommendations also encourage jurisdictions to undertake proactive parallel financial investigations, including by collaborating with public and private financial institutions, as a standard practice when investigating and prosecuting human trafficking crimes, with a view to tracing, freezing, and confiscating proceeds acquired through this crime.

In the United States, the Bank Secrecy Act (BSA) mandates that financial institutions monitor and report suspected illegal activity, such as human trafficking, as well as certain high-dollar cash transactions. The BSA permits financial institutions to share information relevant to money laundering and terrorist financing under the legal safe harbor provided by the USA PATRIOT Act Section 314(b). This reporting and information sharing can be highly useful in tracking and tracing proceeds related to human trafficking.

It is essential that financial institutions train staff on techniques human traffickers use to launder money and the behavioral and financial red flag indicators of human trafficking. Trained customer-facing staff can recognize, document, and report behavioral indicators of human trafficking. Financial institutions are required to comply with law enforcement processes seeking to identify traffickers' assets, which can be seized, forfeited, and used toward restitution for victims. Further, financial institutions can engage with survivors of human trafficking to inform their efforts, including on the development of training programs to enhance the ability of frontline staff and other industry professionals to detect transactions connected to human trafficking, how and when to intervene, and how to determine when a third party is benefitting from the exploitation of another. Consulting with survivors to review existing AML protocols and systems could help to identify gaps and possible improvements.

In 2020, the Government of Canada launched Project PROTECT to increase awareness of sex trafficking, as well as the quantity and quality of suspicious transaction reporting. Canadian financial institutions, FINTRAC (Canada's Financial Intelligence Unit), financial regulators, law enforcement, non-profit organizations, and technology companies collaborated to develop indicia of suspicious transactions of money laundering from sex trafficking. As a result, there was a significant increase in suspicious transaction reports filed by financial institutions related to this activity. FINTRAC disclosed this information to law enforcement to help expand or refine the scope of their cases, uncover new targets, obtain search warrants, and identify assets for seizure or forfeiture. Canadian authorities provided disclosures to counterparts in the United States, the United Kingdom, the Netherlands, Portugal, Jamaica, and Brazil, demonstrating the transnational nature of human trafficking and the importance of international cooperation to end it.

The Role of Technology

Perpetrators use technology in human trafficking schemes. Human trafficking rings often use instant and secure communication mechanisms to facilitate activities among members and employ GPS location applications as one way to remotely control victims.

Technology also can play a critical role in combating these crimes, increase law enforcement's ability to identify victims and perpetrators, and help deliver financial assistance and other victim support services to victims as they work to rebuild their lives.

While human trafficking actors and organizations typically generate illicit proceeds in cash or through the traditional financial system, they sometimes use cryptocurrency. Cryptocurrency transactions, including those involving human trafficking, are recorded on public blockchains. Depending on whether and to what extent anonymizing technologies are applied, blockchain transactions can be analyzed to identify patterns indicative of criminal activity. For example, experts have developed techniques to link some cryptocurrency transaction records to online commercial sex advertisements, which can provide additional information on human trafficking networks. Innovative AML compliance solutions that use big data, advanced analytics, network analysis, and, increasingly, artificial intelligence to monitor transactions and identify and report suspicious transactions can assist governments and the private sector in identifying and combating human trafficking networks.

Traffickers also exploit financial sector innovations, such as prepaid cards and mobile payment applications, to accept payments or move funds through the financial system. Authorities have detected the use of third-party payment processors (TPPPs) by traffickers and their facilitators to wire funds, which gives the appearance that the TPPP is the originator or beneficiary of the wire transfer and conceals the true originator or beneficiary. The use of these innovations leaves digital footprints, which may be detected as these transactions pass through the financial system.

Supporting Survivors of Human Trafficking

Survivors of human trafficking often discover that human traffickers have taken control of their financial identity or banking products and limited or prevented their access to the financial system, spoiling their credit record and hindering their financial reintegration. Financial institutions and civil society can play an important role in assisting survivors in the recovery process by providing them access to digital financial services, such as online microcredit, without requiring traditional identity documentation. Governments can also play a role by supporting the use of digital financial services and innovative tools to assist victims who have been harmed financially. Digital identity solutions and access to digital financial services can help victims securely obtain financial assistance from governments or NGOs, access victim support services, repair their credit, and receive restitution payments when appropriate and available.

Enabling human trafficking survivors' participation in the regulated financial sector is critical. The Liechtenstein Initiative for Finance Against Slavery and Trafficking is a public-private partnership launched in September 2018 to respond to calls from the G7, the G20, the UN General Assembly, and the UN Security Council for governments to partner with the private sector to address human trafficking. Its Survivor Inclusion Initiative works to facilitate survivor access to basic banking services, such as checking and savings accounts by connecting survivors to financial institutions. To support survivors in rebuilding their lives and preventing further exploitation, the financial sector can offer account qualification exception programs and low-to-no fee second chance accounts. Governments, investors, researchers, and civil-society actors should explore how microfinance and other forms of social finance can support survivors.

Periodical and Internet Sources Bibliography

The following articles have been selected to supplement the diverse views presented in this chapter.

Sarah Byrne, "Can New US Law Help Increase Financial Recovery and Reintegration of Survivors of Human Trafficking?" Delta 8.7, January 27, 2022. https://delta87.org/2022/01/can-new-us-law-help-increase-financial-recovery-reintegration-survivors-human-trafficking/.

Penny Crosman, "30 Banks, Nonprofit Team Up to Fight Human Trafficking at Super Bowl," *American Banker*, February 9, 2022. https://www.americanbanker.com/news/30-banks-nonprofit-tech-company-team-up-to-fight-human-trafficking-at-super-bowl.

Sarah Dohoney Byrne, "Financial Institutions are Poised to Take Next Step in Combatting Trafficking," Thomson Reuters, January 11, 2021. https://www.thomsonreuters.com/en-us/posts/investigation-fraud-and-risk/human-trafficking-financial-institutions/.

Jayne Huckerby, "When Human Trafficking and Terrorism Connect: Dangers and Dilemmas," *Just Security*, February 22, 2019. https://www.justsecurity.org/62658/human-trafficking-terrorism-connect-dangers-dilemmas/.

Tom Keatinge, "Disrupting Human Trafficking: The Role of Financial Institutions," Royal United Services Institute, March 14, 2017. https://rusi.org/explore-our-research/publications/whitehall-reports/disrupting-human-trafficking-role-financial-institutions.

Saba Khan, "Q & A: How the Banking Industry Is Fighting Human Trafficking," Children's Hospital of Philadelphia, January 28, 2021. https://policylab.chop.edu/blog/qa-how-banking-industry-fighting-human-trafficking.

Simoney Kyriakou, "HSBC Rolls Out Service to Help Victims of Trafficking," FTAdviser, April 22, 2021. https://www.ftadviser.com/companies/2021/04/22/hsbc-rolls-out-service-to-help-victims-of-trafficking/.

Garret Reich, "The Role Banks and Credit Unions Must Play to Prevent Human Trafficking," the *Financial Brand,* January 17, 2022. https://thefinancialbrand.com/news/bank-culture/banks-credit-unions-prevent-human-trafficking-127820/.

Vicky Shaw, "More Than 1,000 Modern Slavery Victims Helped to Access Bank Accounts," *Independent*, July 21, 2021. https://www.independent.co.uk/money/more-than-1-000-modern-slavery-victims-helped-to-access-bank-accounts-b1887626.html.

Sarah Shearman, "Banks Globally Eye UK Scheme Giving Accounts to Trafficking Survivors," Reuters, March 3, 2020. https://www.reuters.com/article/us-britain-slavery-banking-trfn/banks-globally-eye-uk-scheme-giving-accounts-to-trafficking-survivors-idUSKBN20R0J1.

Chapter 3

What Role Does Technology Play in Human Trafficking?

Chapter Preface

Technology is a ubiquitous part of life in today's society. Many people begin the day by scrolling through their favorite social media sites and connecting with others through messaging or DMs. Hospitals depend upon robotic surgery and a whole array of computerized technology to deliver care. Police departments and other safety agencies use electronic surveillance and other digital tools to enhance their mission of protection and apprehension. The instances of daily technology use are almost endless. In so many ways technology improves our lives. However, it also plays an important role in nefarious enterprises like human trafficking.

Traffickers use technology to attain victims and keep them from escaping the illegal enterprise once they are ensnared. Traffickers also use digital technologies to launder money made from their illicit acts. They are quick to adapt to new forms of technology in order to stay a step ahead of law enforcement. Fortunately, though, law enforcement agencies also find ways to use technology to fight these crimes, and their means of detecting human trafficking with technology are becoming increasingly sophisticated.

This chapter's viewpoints explore these topics. Viewpoints written by the Federal Bureau of Investigation (FBI), Reetika Gupta, Robert W. Gehl, Roderic Broadhurst, and Matthew Bell all analyze the role of the darknet and online platforms that give traffickers an edge for recruiting their victims. The UN Office on Drugs and Crime (UNODC), a crime prevention agency of the United Nations, offers a viewpoint that outlines how traffickers capitalize on digital trends for their illegal activities. Then Tom Simonite and Katie Amodei offer viewpoints that provide information on techniques using digital technology to thwart human traffickers. Through examining the multifaceted role technology plays in facilitating and fighting human trafficking, the viewpoints in this chapter also consider what might be done to help stop it.

Viewpoint 1

> *"FBI investigations show that human traffickers continue to use online platforms to recruit individuals to engage in forced labor or sex work."*

Human Traffickers Recruit Victims Online

Federal Bureau of Investigation

In the following viewpoint, the Federal Bureau of Investigation (FBI) explains how popular digital platforms are being used by human traffickers to recruit victims. The FBI outlines the ways that human traffickers pose as concerned individuals or potential employers to entice victims, and how digital technology has made it easier for traffickers to exploit social media. After providing several examples of people that have been trafficked using online platforms, the FBI gives suggestions on how victims can help law enforcement agencies fight human trafficking. The Federal Bureau of Investigation is the domestic intelligence and security agency of the United States.

As you read, consider the following questions:

1. How do traffickers approach victims online, according to the FBI?
2. What do traffickers promise trafficking victims, as reported by this viewpoint?

"Human Traffickers Continue to Use Popular Online Platforms to Recruit Victims," Federal Bureau of Investigation, March 16, 2020. Reprinted by permission.

3. What kinds of digital information would help law enforcement prosecute traffickers, according to this report?

The FBI warns the public to remain vigilant of the threat posed by criminals who seek to traffic individuals through force, fraud, or coercion through popular social media and dating platforms. Offenders often exploit dating apps and websites to recruit—and later advertise—sex trafficking victims. In addition, offenders are increasingly recruiting labor trafficking victims through what appear to be legitimate job offers.

Definition

The FBI defines human trafficking as compelling someone to engage in labor, services, or a commercial sex act through the use of force, fraud, or coercion.

Methodology

Human trafficking is believed to be the third most prevalent criminal activity in the world. In the United States, people are bought, sold, and smuggled like modern-day slaves. Human trafficking victims are beaten, starved, deceived, and forced into sex work or agricultural, domestic, restaurant, or factory jobs with little to no pay. Many Americans unknowingly encounter trafficking victims through their daily activities.

Traffickers and victims alike come from all different backgrounds: Human trafficking victims have been recovered in rural areas, small towns, the suburbs, and large cities.

FBI investigations show that human traffickers continue to use online platforms to recruit individuals to engage in forced labor or sex work. The Internet lets human traffickers contact virtually anyone in the world, giving them an opportunity to communicate with and recruit victims domestically and internationally. Human traffickers may pose as legitimate job recruiters or agents for modeling companies or employment agencies misrepresenting their true intentions to victims. Traffickers groom victims online by offering opportunities for a better life and providing fake employment opportunities.

Human traffickers target vulnerable individuals by preying on their personal situations. Online platforms make it easier for traffickers to find potential victims, especially those who post personal information, such as their financial hardships, their struggles with low self-esteem, or their family problems. Human traffickers target and recruit their victims by appearing to offer help, or pretending to be a friend or potential romantic partner. They leverage their victims' vulnerabilities and coerce them to meet in person. After establishing a false sense of trust, traffickers may force victims into sex work or forced labor.

Examples

The FBI has identified many examples of traffickers' recruiting individuals using popular online platforms. The following are just a few:

- In July 2019, a Baltimore, Maryland, man was convicted on two counts of sex trafficking of a minor and one count of using the Internet to promote a business enterprise involving prostitution. The perpetrator targeted two girls after they posted information online about their difficult living and financial situation. After meeting them in person, the man forced the two girls into sex work.
- In March 2019, a married couple was found guilty of conspiracy to obtain forced labor and two counts of obtaining forced labor. The couple employed foreign workers to perform domestic labor in their home in Stockton, California. The defendants used the Internet and an India-based newspaper to post false advertisements about the wages and nature of the employment at their home. Upon arrival, the workers were forced to work 18-hour days with little to no wages.

- In October 2017, a sex trafficker was convicted on 17 counts of trafficking adults and minors. Additional charges included child pornography and obstruction of justice. The perpetrator received a 33-year sentence. A victim from the Seattle area met the sex trafficker's accomplice on a dating website. The trafficker and his accomplice later promised to help the victim with her acting career. After a few months, the victim was abused and forced into prostitution.

Victim Reporting

If you believe you or someone you know is the victim of human trafficking of any kind:

Contact your local law enforcement agency, your local FBI field office (contact information can be found at www.fbi.gov), or:

- the National Human Trafficking Hotline—Call 1-888-373-7888 (TTY: 711) or text 233733;
- file a complaint online with the FBI's Internet Crime Complaint Center at www.IC3.gov; or
- contact the FBI's National Threat Operations Center at 1-800-CALL-FBI or tips.fbi.gov.
- To report possible trafficking involving minors, contact the National Center for Missing and Exploited Children (NCMEC) at 1-800-THE-LOST (1-800-843-5678) or at Cybertipline.org.

Victims are encouraged to keep all original documentation, emails, text messages, and logs of communication with the subject. Do not delete anything before law enforcement is able to review it.

Tell law enforcement everything about the online encounters—it may be uncomfortable, but it is necessary to find the offender. When reporting online scams, be as descriptive as possible in the complaint form by providing:

- name and/or user name of the subject;
- email addresses and phone numbers used by the subject;
- websites used by the subject; and

- descriptions of all interactions with the subject.

It is helpful for law enforcement to have as much information as possible to investigate these incidents; however, it is not necessary to provide all of this information to submit a complaint.

The FBI produced this public service announcement to alert Internet users of the continuing threat posed by human traffickers online and what you should do if you or someone you know suspects human trafficking.

Viewpoint 2

> *"Human trafficking is such a major issue, and yet one of the prominent platforms where it takes place is hidden from everyone's eyes on the darknet."*

Human Trafficking Occurs on the Darknet

Reetika Gupta

In the following viewpoint, Reetika Gupta argues that the darknet is a modern-day Silk Road that is used extensively by human traffickers and other criminals. The darknet is an overlay network within the Internet that can only be accessed with authorization or particular software. It allows people to navigate the Internet anonymously. Gupta reports on the criminal activities that take place on the darknet and why traffickers and other criminal types use this market. Finally, Gupta shares why it is difficult to stop this activity. Reetika Gupta is a contributing writer at One Bread Foundation.

As you read, consider the following questions:

1. What does the author describe as the modern-day Silk Road?
2. According to Gupta, what is the darknet?
3. As reported in the viewpoint, why is the darknet used by traffickers and other criminals?

"The Darknet: A Safe Haven for Human Trafficking," by Reetika Gupta, One Bread Foundation, Inc., March 15, 2021. Reprinted by permission.

The Silk Road was an ancient network of trade routes that connected the East and West from the second century to the 18th century. The Silk Road trade played a significant role in the development of the civilizations in those regions, opening long-distance political and economic relations among them.

Wondering Why We Are Talking About It Here?

The Silk Road collapsed in the 18th century. However, it began to operate again in 2011. This time, though, the Silk Road operated as a darknet market—a platform for selling illegal drugs.

Ross Ulbricht, founder of this new Silk Road, was caught and arrested in 2013; however, Silk Road 2.0 emerged afterward. After the FBI shut it down, there was Silk Road 3.0.

This is just the tip of the iceberg. There are multiple operational marketplaces on the darknet. You can hire assassins or sell drugs, arms, sex and humans. That's right—you can sell humans on the darknet!

Human trafficking is such a major issue, and yet one of the prominent platforms where it takes place is hidden from everyone's eyes on the darknet.

This platform is widespread throughout the country. In fact, in the U.S., 2 out of every 3 children sold for sex are trafficked online. It is estimated that 50,000 people in the U.S. alone access the darknet for the sole purpose of trading child pornography.

What Is the Darknet?

As Wharton School of the University of Pennsylvania explains, the darknet is a part of the deep web where the websites are really hard to find, if not impossible. It is used by people who are intentionally trying to hide their identities using specialized software, such as Onion Router or TOR, that hides their Internet Protocol (IP) addresses.

Instead of making direct connections, these software programs allow users to access and communicate using virtual tunnels so that their true locations cannot be identified.

And because identities remain anonymous and untraceable, illegal activities like human trafficking or drug dealing take place unchecked on the darknet.

Using the darknet is not illegal. It is often used to shield classified government activity and protect reform agents, such as human rights activists and journalists, opposed by oppressive foreign regimes.

However, it has emerged as a fully functional marketplace for hidden criminal activity.

Human Trafficking Activities on the Darknet

Criminal organizations have taken to human trafficking on the darknet because it is easy and inexpensive to buy and exploit vulnerable children there. What adds to the misery is that the chance of detection and prosecution of those who are involved in this technology-facilitated human trafficking business is extremely low.

Undoubtedly, the darknet has become a safe haven for human traffickers and pornographers because of these circumstances.

One of the most notorious human trafficking groups, the Black Death Group based out of Eastern Europe, operate on the darknet. Involved with selling sex slaves to Saudi Arabia, it also hosted virgin auctions of girls as young as 15, advertising them by their age, hair color and measurements.

The starting price of an auction can be as high as $762,789. Their disclaimers state they "do not sell girls that are terminally ill, pregnant, have STDs, or are young mothers."

Black Death Group also abducts their victims. They have been accused of kidnapping a 21-year-old British glamor model and mother of one Chloe Ayling, who claimed to be drugged, handcuffed and stuffed in a suitcase while being held captive for six days. Ayling recounted the horrors she experienced to news reporters. She was warned that she would be auctioned to buyers on the darknet and then fed to tigers when they grew bored with her. She was later told she would be auctioned as a sex slave for $354,780.

The Darknet's Connection to Child Pornography

Not only a safe haven for human trafficking, the darknet is the safest and perfect place for child pornography. Many websites allow hundreds of thousands of pedophile members to connect and share tactics on targeting, seducing and engaging in sexual attacks on children.

Efforts to Shut Down the Darknet

The darknet is the perfect platform for criminal activity. Host to anonymous, password-protected sites, the darknet offers anonymity to illicit vendors and customers to conduct their business online, which makes policing this online space complicated.

Despite the best efforts of the government, the intricate nature of the deep web makes it very difficult to trace users. Though law enforcement agencies have been continuously working to stop these activities, there are huge numbers of people who operate on the darknet, which makes it difficult for the agencies to investigate and prosecute them.

As decent human beings, it is our duty to show empathy toward one another. If someone today is being exploited, then tomorrow it may happen to us as well. It is important that we join hands to help each other, educate each other and take steps to end human trafficking. To read more about this issue and learn how you can help abolish child sex trafficking, read more of our blogs and share them with your family and friends.

Viewpoint 3

> *"Social networks and smartphones have enabled new forms of commerce and fun—but also made it easier to traffic in children or pornographic material featuring them."*

Using Facial Recognition Technology Can Help Prevent Child Sex Trafficking

Tom Simonite

In the following viewpoint, Tom Simonite reports on the use of facial recognition and other digital technologies to fight child sex trafficking. These tools use algorithms to look for common signs of child abuse and trafficking in images and texts. This can then help investigators track down child traffickers. Simonite reviews several technological tools and projects that are being deployed by tech companies in the fight against child sex trafficking and provides examples where law enforcement successfully rescued children from trafficking. With this new model, investigators do not have to wait for companies or users to report child trafficking and abuse and can act quickly. Simonite is a senior editor for business coverage at Wired.

As you read, consider the following questions:

1. According to the author, what is Spotlight?
2. What is Thorn, as reported in this viewpoint?

"How Facial Recognition Is Fighting Child Sex Trafficking," by Tom Simonite, Wired, July 19, 2019. Reprinted by permission.

3. What system does the Safer technology use, as explained by Simonite?

One evening in April, a California law enforcement officer was browsing Facebook when she saw a post from the National Center for Missing and Exploited Children with a picture of a missing child. The officer took a screenshot of the image, which she later fed into a tool created by nonprofit Thorn to help investigators find underage sex-trafficking victims. The tool, called Spotlight, uses text- and image-processing algorithms to match faces and other clues in online sex ads with other evidence.

Using Amazon's facial recognition technology, Spotlight quickly returned a list of online sex ads featuring the girl's photo. She had been sold for weeks. The ads set in motion some more traditional police work. "Within weeks that child was recovered and removed from trauma," Julie Cordua, CEO of Thorn, said, recounting the case at an Amazon conference in Las Vegas this month.

The rescue illustrates Thorn's strategy of nurturing new technology to combat child sex-trafficking and exploitation online. The nonprofit was cofounded in 2009 by actors Demi Moore and Ashton Kutcher and has become influential with both law enforcement—who can use Spotlight and other tools for free—and the tech industry. Thorn's partners include Facebook, Amazon, and Dropbox.

Thorn may soon expand its influence. In April, the nonprofit was named one of eight projects that will share in $280 million from TED's philanthropic offshoot, the Audacious Project. Thorn's exact share has not been disclosed, but it will likely provide a major boost: The nonprofit's income totaled $3.2 million in 2017, filings show.

One potential use for the new funding: new technology that would dig deeper into the online supply chain of child pornography, attempting to control it closer to the source. Cordua imagines software crawling the dark web, where she says the material often first appears, to find new imagery. Digital fingerprints for the files could then be added to automated blacklists used by companies such as Facebook, preventing it from circulating more broadly. Facebook says it took action on 5.4 million pieces of child pornography in the first quarter of 2019.

Cordua describes Thorn's mission as a kind of immune response to an undertreated disease of the internet. Social networks and smartphones have enabled new forms of commerce and fun—but also made it easier to traffic in children or pornographic material featuring them. Cops lack the tools and expertise needed to fight that, Cordua says. Tech companies lack the motivation to spend heavily on a problem where progress doesn't offer profits.

"It was becoming more and more difficult to address this problem," Cordua says. She previously led global marketing at Motorola's cellphone division during the brand's peak, and filled a similar role at RED, the brand Apple and others use to direct funds to AIDS programs in Africa.

Thorn initially worked to pressure technology companies to do more about online child exploitation. More recently, it shifted to what Cordua says is a more effective strategy of producing and operating new technology for use by law enforcement and the private sector.

Spotlight was Thorn's first software project and got its first major test during the 2015 Super Bowl, in Arizona. The initial version used text processing technology to highlight posts likely to be written by, or about, an underage person, and to pull out phone numbers and other data. Investigators could use those details to connect different ads, or cross-reference with NCMEC's list of missing children.

Spotlight had been built on Amazon's cloud service from an early stage, but in 2018 the two organizations began to talk about new features that use the company's image processing technology. Investigators can now use facial recognition algorithms marketed under Amazon's Rekognition service to check images against faces on NCMEC's list. Spotlight also uses Rekognition to extract text from photos, because some sex ads hide text in images to escape conventional search tools.

Thorn says Spotlight has been used by law enforcement on almost 40,000 cases in North America, in which investigators found more than 9,000 children, and over 10,000 traffickers. For Amazon, Thorn also offers a way to highlight the benefits of facial recognition, after accusations that its use by law enforcement endangers privacy, and that the company's technology is inaccurate.

Thorn's second major software product, Safer, is built around different image processing technology. It helps tech companies detect images of child sexual abuse on their platforms using PhotoDNA, a system developed by Microsoft with Dartmouth College, and used by other companies including Facebook.

PhotoDNA works by checking images against a list of hashes—mathematical fingerprints—of known child-abuse images. Cordua says Thorn's implementation makes deploying the system and processes needed to support it less costly, encouraging use by smaller firms. Photo sharing sites Imgur and SmugMug, which owns Flickr, are among a handful of companies testing Safer.

Cordua says the new investment from TED's Project Audacity could help make hashing blacklists more proactive, so images can be added to the system before they have circulated widely. That requires digging into the dark web—sites protected by anonymity tools such as Tor.

"The dream scenario is that in real time you could get hashes from newly produced content from the dark web, before it goes viral," Cordua says. The plan is still taking shape, but one option would be to train machine learning algorithms that could flag potential material for review by experts. Thorn has previously built language processing tools to help law enforcement officers find child abuse content on the dark web.

Thorn has been in talks with the Canadian Centre for Child Protection, a fellow nonprofit, about coordinating to curtail child pornography on the dark web. The Canadian organization operates software called Project Arachnid that crawls the dark web and conventional websites to spot known child abuse images and automatically notify site operators. It also helps investigators find new content. In two and a half years, Arachnid has crawled 76 billion images, and sent out 3.8 million notices.

Hany Farid, a UC Berkeley professor who codeveloped PhotoDNA with Microsoft while at Dartmouth, says that program has demonstrated an important new model for tackling child pornography. Previous work has typically waited for companies or users to report material. “This is the first and only active approach, as far as I know,” Farid says. He also says Thorn has experience tracking content beyond the openly accessible web. “Thorn has been effective at diving into the dark web where a lot of child sexual abuse material has moved,” he says.

Lianna McDonald, executive director at the Canadian organization, says a new generation of more proactive technical tools can take the fight to suppress child exploitation online to a new level. “We’re at a point where we really feel that we’re going to get ahead of this victimization,” she says.

Viewpoint 4

> *"Hotel managers can use new technology tools to add reminders for staff to remember to watch for human trafficking."*

Hotels Can Use Technology to Prevent Human Trafficking

Katie Amodei

In the following viewpoint, Katie Amodei analyzes how new technology that was implemented by hotels during the COVID-19 pandemic can help prevent human trafficking. Amodei argues that with the correct training, hotel staff can be agents of change and intervene in human sex trafficking. Amodei outlines ways that hotels are using new technologies and combining them with the traditional services provided at hotels to spot potential cases of trafficking. For example, hotel security departments are able to watch for potential signs of trafficking in guest activity using new technology. Katie Amodei is the communications manager for the nonprofit Businesses Ending Slavery and Trafficking.

As you read, consider the following questions:

1. As reported by Amodei, what is Alice?
2. What are two of the contactless technologies Amodei references in this viewpoint?

"How Contactless Technology Can Prevent Human Trafficking," by Katie Amodei, Hotel Management, March 10, 2021. Reprinted by permission.

3. According to this viewpoint, what is one sign that trafficking may be occurring?

The coronavirus pandemic has forced hotels to change their operations. When the pandemic began, many hoteliers worried that switching to using technology systems that require less face-to-face contact could result in guests missing out on what makes hospitality special—the personal touch. But as we move into the second year of the pandemic, hotels are finding that contactless technology is not reducing the guest experience. In fact, technology is allowing more touchpoints with guests while streamlining task management for employees.

Even before the pandemic, new technology trends like keyless entry and self-check-in were already becoming popular in the hospitality industry. The pandemic has accelerated the popularity of contactless technology, and many hotels are discovering that implementing digitalization is changing hospitality for the better.

"There has always been a fear that automation would replace the human touch, so this was seen as a threat to staff," said Aileen Jimenez, associate product manager for Alice, which provides a global operations platform specifically for the hospitality industry. "But what we are finding is that hotels are seeing a lot of positives coming from new technology."

Messaging

One positive is guest messaging. Before the guest even arrives at the hotel, they can receive a text message welcoming them and asking if there is anything the hotel staff can do to make the guest's stay better. Then throughout the stay, guest messaging allows staff to check-in with the guest to ask about their needs. Guests can text back a wide range of requests, from requesting more towels to asking staff to help schedule a tennis match. Once the guest responds to an automated text message, it can be a staff member, not a computer automation, responding. This is helping hotels not only continue to meet guest needs during the COVID-19 pandemic, but hoteliers are understanding their guests needs better than ever because they are able to collect data that, over time, shows trends with their guests.

Hotels using Alice's platform are seeing a shift with how guests are connecting with staff. "They are still able to provide the human touch—just in a different way," Jimenez said. "Now, because of COVID, guests are appreciating more privacy. They really like the convenience of self-check-in and keyless entry, and there is increased engagement with texting."

Blockchain Can Help Fight Human Trafficking

The granddaughter of Queen Elizabeth, Princess Eugenie as well as the United States Ambassador for Anti-Human Trafficking John Richmond both showed their vote of confidence about using technology such as mobile apps as well as Blockchain to address the serious issue of human trafficking.

Increased Internet Usage for Human Trafficking

The OSCE (Organization for Security and Co-Operation in Europe) hosted the conference in Vienna, Austria where the Princess and Ambassador Richmond spoke. It was during this conference that experts in the field stated that the increase in the use of the internet had also given human traffickers a greater opportunity to exploit possible targets.

Princess Eugenie was the person who pointed out that modern technology could also be used to help fight this evil. The Princess is the co-founder of the Anti-Slavery Collective, an initiative focused on creating awareness about and also abolishing modern slavery.

In her speech she said that she had learned about how Blockchain technology was having a significant impact on supply-

Hospitality software platforms are also helping with back of house, decreasing the number of times employees must meet in person with their managers or other employees, creating a streamlined operations process that delivers efficiency and allows for social distancing as work tasks are assigned and completed through a digital platform instead of using paper checklists. For example, by using devices, housekeepers can easily update a room's status to be ready for inspection, and every team member can instantly see the status in real time, while other staff members can easily let housekeeping know which rooms are vacant and ready to be cleaned.

chain management. She added that she also came to know about how an app in Britain could help the public report modern slavery that was taking place at car washes.

Ambassador Richmond also noted that while technology on its own could not put a stop to human trafficking, it could be used to create tools that can help in the fight against this evil.

Using Blockchain to End Forced Labor

The app the Princess was referring to was created for a joint initiative by the Coca Cola Co., the US Department of State as well as the Safe Car Wash app. This initiative was launched in March last year, and its focus has been to use Blockchain technology to create a secured work registry.

The Safe Car Wash App was launched in June last year via a partnership between the Catholic Church in England and Wales and the Church of England after the organizations found that there were almost 1,000 cases of forced or slave labor at car washes across the United Kingdom.

"Blockchain Can Help Against Human Trafficking," Chainbits, September 4, 2019.

Preventing Trafficking

With the pandemic pushing more hotels to embrace the contactless experience, combined with the popularity of how efficient these new systems are for both guests and employees, the digitizing of hotels is a trend that is here to stay well after the pandemic ends. But many hoteliers are concerned that their staff will have fewer opportunities to spot or prevent situations involving human trafficking. With the accelerated shift toward contactless technologies, the opportunities to prevent human trafficking are also shifting.

Hotel managers can use new technology tools to add reminders for staff to remember to watch for human trafficking or add a list of human trafficking indicators that staff can access through their devices. In addition, managers can easily assign times for employees to receive online human trafficking awareness training, especially if the link to the training is inserted directly into each employee's tasks.

Security departments are vital for preventing human trafficking, especially when guests are having less face-to-face contact with other employees—security departments are the eyes in the sky. Don Cohen, director of security at a large hotel, recommends security departments continuously train for ways to help watch for and prevent human trafficking. "Having a well-trained team that knows how to work together and making sure everyone knows the standard operating procedures is really important," Cohen said. "We have built human trafficking training right into our safety training, and we have human trafficking prevention signage and literature in back-of-house areas so staff know what to do if they see something suspicious."

According to Cohen, security departments can leverage the use of new technology to help them identify human trafficking. A benefit of using a hospitality software platform is that security departments can monitor guestroom door activity. Platforms can report how often a door opens, and they even show if it was opened by keyless entry from the outside or if the door is opened from the inside. When security staff see that a door is opened an uncommon number of times—that can be a warning sign for security.

Technology can also help security departments control who has access to elevators. This is important for regulating the number of people who are not guests at the hotel from accessing rooms by requiring visitors to have either a guest or a hotel employee allow them access to the elevators from the lobby.

Guest messaging can also be a powerful tool for helping human trafficking victims. If a victim is in control of a smartphone and is able to communicate with hotel staff, he or she can text staff to ask for help without drawing attention from his or her abusers. On the flip side, if a staff member is concerned about a particular guest, he or she can text to make sure everything is OK and invite the guest to reach out if in need of help or assistance. This type of human trafficking intervention can be safer for both the victim and the staff member as long as it is framed as a customer service check that is done for all guests.

These new technology systems are the wave of the future for the hospitality industry. At first glance it may seem that less human contact in hotels might make guests feel isolated or make spotting human trafficking more difficult, but if hotels are intentional about how they go digital, there are ways hoteliers can use technology to increase touchpoints with guests, foster better employee communication and keep hotels safe from both COVID-19 and traffickers.

Viewpoint 5

> *"Research conducted by the UN Office on Drugs and Crime (UNODC) shows how victims are being targeted and recruited via social media and online dating platforms, where personal information and details of people's locations are readily available."*

Traffickers Capitalize on Online Technology

The United Nations Office on Drugs and Crime

In the following viewpoint, the United Nations Office on Drugs and Crime (UNODC) analyzes the insidious connection between digital technologies and human trafficking. The UNODC maintains that traffickers use both social media and dating platforms to easily find their victims. UNODC then demonstrates how traffickers exploit different digital technologies to keep control of victims, sell and distribute sexually abusive videos, hide money in cryptocurrencies, and hide their identities from the authorities. UNODC is an agency of the United Nations that focuses on crime prevention, criminal justice, drug trafficking, terrorism, and political corruption.

As you read, consider the following questions:

1. According to the UN, how is the dark web used by traffickers?
2. What is the most common place for recruiting trafficking victims, as stated in this viewpoint?
3. As reported in the viewpoint, how did COVID-19 affect trafficking?

Human traffickers who trick people with fake job offers and promises and then exploit them for profit, are taking advantage of online technologies for every step of their criminal activities.

Research conducted by the UN Office on Drugs and Crime (UNODC) shows how victims are being targeted and recruited via social media and online dating platforms, where personal information and details of people's locations are readily available.

Sexual abuse and other forms of exploitation are taking place virtually and photos and videos sold further on different platforms to customers worldwide, resulting in even more money for the traffickers at no additional cost.

New Strategies

This week, experts from around 100 countries met online and in Vienna, Austria, to discuss strategies to combat this phenomenon and make the best use of technology to prevent human trafficking and investigate cases of this crime.

The discussion formed part of the annual intergovernmental Working Group of Trafficking in Persons and centres around an in-depth background paper on this topic produced by UNODC's Human Trafficking and Migrant Smuggling Section.

"Traffickers are quick to adapt their business model to suit their needs and increase their profits, so of course they follow online trends," explains Tiphanie Crittin, a UNODC Crime Prevention and Criminal Justice Officer.

Dark Web Exploitation

"Traffickers are currently using technology to profile, recruit, control and exploit their victims as well as using the Internet, especially the dark web, to hide illegal materials stemming from trafficking and their real identities from investigators."

The illicit proceeds from this highly profitable crime are also being laundered online through crypto currencies, which makes it easier for traffickers to receive, hide and move large amounts of money with less risk of being detected.

Today, the Internet provides easy access to a much larger group of potential victims because traditional physical and geographical limitations no longer exist.

Traffickers create fake websites or post advertisements on legitimate employment portals and social networking websites.

Live Chat Scams

Some of these sites feature the option of a live chat. This gives the trafficker immediate contact and the opportunity to obtain personal information, such as passport details, enhancing their power over the targeted victims.

Victims can be repeatedly exploited through live streaming on multiple websites, and there is no limit on the number of times videos of their abuse may be viewed and by how many people.

The global nature of human trafficking and the abuse of technology makes it even more difficult for law enforcement authorities to tackle this crime, explains Ms. Crittin.

"When a crime is planned in one country, with victims in another country, and a customer in a third one, law enforcement authorities face practical challenges such as finding and securing evidence, as any investigation requires cooperation across borders and a certain level of digital expertise," she says.

Remote Control

Traffickers use technology to control their victims remotely, sometimes without having to ever met them in person.

Location-tracking applications and use of global positioning systems in mobile phones can be used to know the victim's location, while cameras in smartphones used during video calls enable traffickers to see their victims and their surroundings.

Traffickers also maintain control over their victims by threatening to release intimate photos or videos of them to families and friends if they do not comply with their demands.

One of the panellists at the Working Group, Alexandra Gelber, the Deputy Chief for Policy and Legislation at the Child Exploitation and Obscenity Section of the United States' Department of Justice, highlighted the links between trafficking and online technology in her country.

Online Marketplace

"Data shows that in the United States approximately 40% of sex trafficking victims are recruited online, making the Internet the most common place where victim recruitment takes place," she says.

"For over a decade, online advertising has been the main tactic used by traffickers to solicit buyers for commercial sex. In 2020, over 80% of the [Justice Department's] sex trafficking prosecutions involved online advertising."

Ms. Gelber adds that technology is also being used to commit "virtual child sex trafficking" which takes place when an offender in the United States sends a digital payment to a trafficker in another country.

"The trafficker will then sexually abuse a child in front of a web camera, while the offender in the United States watches a livestream of the abuse."

COVID Factor

The COVID-19 pandemic has provided further opportunities for traffickers due to the increased use of the Internet, in particular social networks and online video gaming sites.

"Containment measures to control the spread of the virus meant that people spent much more time online, especially children since schools were closed. We have seen an increase in child sexual exploitation materials created and shared online during the pandemic," says Tiphanie Crittin.

Despite the increasing criminal uses of technology by traffickers, technology can also be used to identify victims and support police investigations and prosecutions.

Stricter Frameworks Needed

"However, when investigators enter the digital world of citizens, they have access to personal information. It is crucial to have strict frameworks around such access and use of data to make sure that the right to privacy and human rights are respected," says UNODC's Ms. Crittin.

The UNODC background paper shares numerous examples of existing or promising partnerships and tools which countries are using or developing. These include digital forensics, data scanning tools, smartphone apps and successful collaborations with technology, social media and Internet companies.

UNODC has also co-organized "DataJams" with computing giant IBM and the Colombian non-governmental organization Pasos Libres, in which students compete online to develop technology-based solutions to identify and protect victims of trafficking and support prosecutions.

VIEWPOINT 

> *"Given the often sensationalized media coverage of the dark web, it's understandable that people think the term 'dark' is a moral judgment."*

The Dark Web Has Dangers and Benefits

Robert W. Gehl

In this viewpoint, Robert W. Gehl argues that although the dark web—sometimes known as the darknet—gets a bad reputation for facilitating illegal activity such as human trafficking, it has many legitimate uses as well that shouldn't be overshadowed. The dark web offers users more privacy and anonymity, which can help facilitate crimes but also protects user data in a way that the regular Internet does not. Gehl also points out that a large amount of online criminal activity actually happens on the regular Internet. Robert W. Gehl is an associate professor of communication at the University of Utah and author of Weaving the Dark Web: Legitimacy on Freenet, Tor, and I2P.

As you read, consider the following questions:

1. According to this viewpoint, what is the difference between dark websites and regular websites?
2. How does Gehl define "going dark"?
3. What does Gehl say is the risk of negative inaccurate assumptions about the dark web?

"Illuminating the 'dark web,'" by Robert W. Gehl, The Conversation, October 30, 2018. https://theconversation.com/illuminating-the-dark-web-105542.

In the wake of recent violent events in the U.S., many people are expressing concern about the tone and content of online communications, including talk of the "dark web." Despite the sinister-sounding phrase, there is not just one "dark web." The term is actually fairly technical in origin, and is often used to describe some of the lesser-known corners of the internet. As I discuss in my new book, "Weaving the Dark Web: Legitimacy on Freenet, Tor, and I2P," the online services that make up what has become called the "dark web" have been evolving since the early days of the commercial internet – but because of their technological differences, are not well understood by the public, policymakers or the media.

As a result, people often think of the dark web as a place where people sell drugs or exchange stolen information – or as some rare section of the internet Google can't crawl. It's both, and neither, and much more.

Seeking Anonymity and Privacy

In brief, dark websites are just like any other website, containing whatever information its owners want to provide, and built with standard web technologies, like hosting software, HTML and JavaScript. Dark websites can be viewed by a standard web browser like Firefox or Chrome. The difference is that they can only be accessed through special network-routing software, which is designed to provide anonymity for both visitors to websites and publishers of these sites.

Websites on the dark web don't end in ".com" or ".org" or other more common web address endings; they more often include long strings of letters and numbers, ending in ".onion" or ".i2p." Those are signals that tell software like Freenet, I2P or Tor how to find dark websites while keeping users' and hosts' identities private.

Those programs got their start a couple of decades ago. In 1999, Irish computer scientist Ian Clarke started Freenet as a peer-to-peer system for computers to distribute various types of data in a decentralized manner rather than through the more centralized structure of the mainstream internet. The structure of Freenet separates the identity of the creator of a file from its content, which made it attractive for people who wanted to host anonymous websites.

Not long after Freenet began, the Tor Project and the Invisible Internet Project developed their own distinct methods for anonymously hosting websites.

Today, the more commonly used internet has billions of websites – but the dark web is tiny, with tens of thousands of sites at the most, at least according to the various indexes and search engines that crawl these three networks.

A More Private Web

The most commonly used of the three anonymous systems is Tor – which is so prominent that mainstream websites like Facebook, *The New York Times* and *The Washington Post* operate versions of their websites accessible on Tor's network. Obviously, those sites don't seek to keep their identities secret, but they have piggybacked on Tor's anonymizing web technology in order to allow users to connect privately and securely without governments knowing.

In addition, Tor's system is set up to allow users to anonymously browse not only dark websites, but also regular websites. Using Tor to access the regular internet privately is much more common than using it to browse the dark web.

Moral Aspects of 'Dark' Browsing

Given the often sensationalized media coverage of the dark web, it's understandable that people think the term "dark" is a moral judgment. Hitmen for hire, terrorist propaganda, child trafficking and exploitation, guns, drugs and stolen information markets do sound pretty dark.

Yet people commit crimes throughout the internet with some regularity – including trying to hire killers on Craigslist and using Venmo to pay for drug purchases. One of the activities often associated with the dark web, terrorist propaganda, is far more prevalent on the regular web.

Defining the dark web only by the bad things that happen there ignores the innovative search engines and privacy-conscious social networking – as well as important blogging by political dissidents.

Even complaining that dark web information isn't indexed by search engines misses the crucial reality that search engines never see huge swaths of the regular internet either – such as email traffic, online gaming activity, streaming video services, documents shared within corporations or on data-sharing services like Dropbox, academic and news articles behind paywalls, interactive databases and even posts on social media sites. Ultimately, though, the dark web is indeed searchable as I explain in a chapter of my book.

Thus, as I suggest, a more accurate connotation of "dark" in "dark web" is found in the phrase "going dark" – moving communications out of clear and public channels and into encrypted or more private ones.

Managing Anxieties

Focusing all this fear and moral judgment on the dark web risks both needlessly scaring people about online safety and erroneously reassuring them about online safety.

For instance, the financial services company Experian sells services that purport to "monitor the dark web" to alert customers when their personal data has been compromised by hackers and offered for sale online. Yet to sign up for that service, customers have to give the company all sorts of personal information – including their Social Security number and email address – the very data they're seeking to protect. And they have to hope that Experian doesn't get hacked, as its competitor Equifax was, compromising the personal data of nearly every adult in the U.S.

It's inaccurate to assume that online crime is based on the dark web – or that the only activity on the dark web is dangerous and illegal. It's also inaccurate to see the dark web as content beyond the reach of search engines. Acting on these incorrect assumptions would encourage governments and corporations to want to monitor and police online activity – and risk giving public support to privacy-invading efforts.

"The Tor Project's developers have acknowledged the potential to misuse the service which, when combined with technologies such as untraceable cryptocurrency, can help hide criminals."

The Dark Web Facilitates Child Exploitation

Roderic Broadhurst and Matthew Bell

In this viewpoint, Roderic Broadhurst and Matthew Bell argue that the dark web—also known as the darknet—helps facilitate the production and distribution of a large amount of material involving child exploitation and abuse. The Tor network is among the biggest contributors to this problem. Although undercover operations targeting child abuse and human trafficking have had some success infiltrating forums on Tor, much more needs to be done to prevent material that supports child abuse and trafficking from spreading on the darknet. Roderic Broadhurst is a professor of criminology at the School of Global Governance and Regulation of the College of Asia and the Pacific. Matthew Bell is Laboratory Coordinator at the Australian National University's Cybercrime Observatory.

"How the world's biggest dark web platform spreads millions of items of child sex abuse material — and why it's hard to stop," Roderic Broadhurst and Matthew Bell, The Conversation, September 2, 2021. https://theconversation.com/how-the-worlds-biggest-dark-web-platform-spreads-millions-of-items-of-child-sex-abuse-material-and-why-its-hard-to-stop-167107.

As you read, consider the following questions:

1. According to this viewpoint, what are the two technologies that Tor overlays?
2. According to data cited in this viewpoint, what percent of Tor domains contain legal content?
3. According to the authors, what makes it difficult to prosecute people who produce and distribute child abuse and exploitation material online?

Child sexual abuse material is rampant online, despite considerable efforts by big tech companies and governments to curb it. And according to reports, it has only become more prevalent during the COVID-19 pandemic.

This material is largely hosted on the anonymous part of the internet — the "darknet" — where perpetrators can share it with little fear of prosecution. There are currently a few platforms offering anonymous internet access, including i2p, FreeNet and Tor.

Tor is by far the largest and presents the biggest conundrum. The open-source network and browser grants users anonymity by encrypting their information and letting them escape tracking by internet service providers.

Online privacy advocates including Edward Snowden have championed the benefits of such platforms, claiming they protect free speech, freedom of thought and civil rights. But they have a dark side, too.

Tor's Perverted Underworld

The Tor Project was initially developed by the US Navy to protect online intelligence communications, before its code was publicly released in 2002. The Tor Project's developers have acknowledged the potential to misuse the service which, when combined with technologies such as untraceable cryptocurrency, can help hide criminals.

Tor is an overlay network that exists "on top" of the internet and merges two technologies. The first is the onion service software.

These are the websites, or "onion services", hosted on the Tor network. These sites require an onion address and their servers' physical locations are hidden from users.

The second is Tor's privacy-maximising browser. It enables users to browse the internet anonymously by hiding their identity and location. While the Tor browser is needed to access onion services, it can also be used to browse the "surface" internet.

Accessing the Tor network is simple. And while search engine options are limited (there's no Google), discovering onion services is simple, too. The BBC, New York Times, ProPublica, Facebook, the CIA and Pornhub all have a verified presence on Tor, to name a few.

Service dictionaries such as "The Hidden Wiki" list addresses on the network, allowing users to discover other (often illicit) services.

Child Sex Abuse Material and Abuse Porn Is Prevalent

The number of onion services active on the Tor network is unknown, although the Tor Project estimates about 170,000 active addresses. The architecture of the network allows partial monitoring of the network traffic and a summary of which services are visited. Among the visited services, child sex abuse material is common.

Of the estimated 2.6 million users that use the Tor network daily, one study reported only 2% (52,000) of users accessed onion services. This suggests most users access the network to retain their online privacy, rather than use anonymous onion services.

That said, the same study found from a single data capture that about 80% of traffic to onion services was directed to services which did offer illegal porn, abuse images and/or child sex abuse material.

Another study estimated 53.4% of the 170,000 or so active onion domains contained legal content, suggesting 46.6% of services had content which was either illegal, or in a grey area.

Although scams make up a significant proportion of these services, cryptocurrency services, drug deals, malware, weapons, stolen credentials, counterfeit products and child sex abuse material also feature in this dark part of the internet.

Only about 7.5% of the child sex abuse material on the Tor network is estimated to be sold for a profit. The majority of those involved aren't in it for money, so most of this material is simply swapped. That said, some services have started charging fees for content.

Several high-profile onion services hosting child sex abuse material have been shut down following extensive cross-jurisdictional law enforcement operations, including The Love Zone website in 2014, PlaypEn in 2015 and Child's Play in 2017.

A recent effort led by German police, and involving others including Australian Federal Police, Europol and the FBI, resulted in the shutdown of the illegal website Boystown in May.

But one of the largest child sex abuse material forums on the internet (not just Tor) has evaded law enforcement (and activist) takedown attempts for a decade. As of last month it had 508,721 registered users. And since 2013 it has hosted over a million pictures and videos of child sex abuse material and abuse porn.

The paedophile (eroticisation of pre-pubescent children), haebephile (pubescent children) and ephebophile (adolescents) communities are among the early adopters of anonymous discussion forums on Tor. Forum members distribute media, support each other and exchange tips to avoid police detection and scams targeting them.

The WeProtect Alliance's 2019 Global Threat Assessment report estimated there were more than 2.88 million users on ten forums dedicated to paedophilia and paraphilia interests operating via onion services.

Countermeasures

There are huge challenges for law enforcement trying to prosecute those who produce and/or distribute child sex abuse material online. Such criminal activity typically falls across multiple jurisdictions, making detection and prosecution difficult.

Undercover operations and novel online investigative techniques are essential. One example is targeted "hacks" which offer law enforcement back-door access to sites or forums hosting child sex abuse material.

Such operations are facilitated by cybercrime and transnational organised crime treaties which address child sex abuse material and the trafficking of women and children.

Given the volatile nature of many onion services, a focus on onion directories and forums may help with harm reduction. Little is known about child sex abuse material forums on Tor, or the extent to which they influence onion services hosting this material.

Apart from coordinating to avoid detection, forum users can also share information about police activity, rate onion service vendors, share sites and expose scams targeting them.

The monitoring of forums by outsiders can lead to actionable interventions, such as the successful profiling of active offenders. Some agencies have explored using undercover law enforcement officers, civil society, or NGO experts (such as from the WeProtect Global Alliance or ECPAT International) to promote self-regulation within these groups.

While there is a lack of research on this, reformed or recovering offenders can also provide counsel to others. Some sub-forums seek to offer education, encourage treatment and reduce harm — usually by focusing on the legal and health issues associated with consuming child sex abuse material, and ways to control urges and avoid stimuli.

Other contraband services also play a role. For instance, onion services dedicated to drug, malware or other illicit trading usually ban child sex abuse material that creeps in.

Why does the Tor network allow such abhorrent material to remain, despite extensive opposition — sometimes even from those within these groups? Surely those representing Tor have read complaints in the media, if not survivor reports about child sex abuse material.

Viewpoint 8

> *"There is an opportunity – albeit a challenging one – to use the bits of information we can get on the distribution of victims, traffickers, buyers and exploiters, and disrupt the supply chain wherever and however we can."*

Data Science Technology Can Help Stop Human Trafficking

Renata Konrad and Andrew C. Trapp

In this viewpoint by Renata Konrad and Andrew C. Trapp, the authors argue that data analytics could be used to help prevent human trafficking. This involves looking at the data trail of traffickers and their victims in order to interrupt the trafficking process. Analytics can also make use of face-recognition software to find ads from traffickers on social media and other websites. Through developing network analysis and analytics, data science can be used to help law enforcement identify patterns in human trafficking. Renata Konrad is an assistant professor of operations and industrial engineering at Worcester University, and Andrew C. Trapp is an associate professor in the same department.

As you read, consider the following questions:

1. What are the risk factors for human trafficking mentioned in this viewpoint?
2. According to this viewpoint, what is machine learning and how could it be applied to fighting human trafficking?
3. According to the authors, what is a challenge to network interruption in some countries?

July 30 marks the United Nations' World Day Against Trafficking in Persons, a day focused on ending the criminal exploitation of children, women and men for forced labor or sex work.

Between 27 and 45.8 million individuals worldwide are trapped in some form of modern-day slavery. The victims are forced into slavery as sex workers, beggars and child soldiers, or as domestic workers, factory workers and laborers in manufacturing, construction, mining, commercial fishing and other industries.

Human trafficking occurs in every country in the world, including the U.S. It's a hugely profitable industry, generating an estimated US$150 billion annually in illegal profits per year. In fact, it's one of the largest sources of profit for global organized crime, second only to illicit drugs.

Analytics, the mathematical search for insights in data, could help law enforcement combat human trafficking. Human trafficking is essentially a supply chain in which the "supply" (human victims) moves through a network to meet "demand" (for cheap, vulnerable and illegal labor). Traffickers leave a data trail, however faint or broken, despite their efforts to operate off the grid and in the shadows.

There is an opportunity – albeit a challenging one – to use the bits of information we can get on the distribution of victims, traffickers, buyers and exploiters, and disrupt the supply chain wherever and however we can. In our latest study, we have detailed how this might work.

Finding People at Risk

In most countries, resources to fight human trafficking are woefully inadequate. Agencies strive to use them as effectively and efficiently as possible, and often find themselves fighting for scarce funding and support. A government, for example, may need to decide how best to fund or schedule labor inspectors to detect child labor in the manufacturing industry. An organization with limited resources may need insight into which prevention program to run, or what type of awareness campaign to implement.

We can use data to identify populations most at-risk and target prevention campaigns to those populations. Risk factors for being drawn into trafficking include poverty, unemployment, migration and escape from political conflict or war. Experiences with organized crime and natural disasters can also change to a person's risk.

Trafficking often begins with fraudulent recruitment methods, such as promises of employment or romance. Data can help identify specific economically depressed areas, where we can deploy awareness campaigns and social service support.

In operations research, scientists apply mathematical methods to answer complex questions about patterns in data and predict future trends or behaviors. Analytical tools similar to those used in transportation, manufacturing and finance can help us decide where to best allocate resources and help locate shelters for victims.

Victim Identification and Location

Trafficking networks are dynamic. Traffickers are likely to frequently change distribution and transportation routes to avoid detection, leaving law enforcement and analysts with incomplete information as they attempt to identify and dismantle trafficking networks.

However, researchers can help by tracking subtle trends in data at various locations; at access points where we actually come in contact with victims, such as the emergency room; and in the activity of local law enforcement.

In the sex trade, for example, clues may be found in patterns of petty theft, by looking at transactional data from purchases at retail outlets. Victims sometimes steal essential supplies that traffickers may not provide for them such as feminine hygiene products, soap and toothpaste. Trends in the use of cash for transactions normally made with debit or credit cards – hotel bookings, for example – may also raise a red flag.

Traffickers advertise on social media and internet-based sites. Analytics could seek patterns in photos through facial recognition software, comparing images from missing person reports or trafficking ads.

Sex trafficking activity, in particular, leaves traces in the public areas of the internet, mostly in the form of advertisements and escort ads. Advertisers tend to use social networks and dating websites, while more proficient traffickers frequently alter their online presence to try to elude identification.

Machine learning – a type of artificial intelligence where computers teach themselves to do tasks, such as recognize images – can be used to detect online trafficking activity. Recent advances in matrix completion, a type of machine learning, could even help clean up falsified information or make predictions about missing data.

Traffickers are also known to take advantage of increased demand for commercial sexual exploitation during major events, including conventions and large sporting events. Analyses that look at both location and timing of online ads could help law enforcement detect and possibly interdict transportation of victims to the event. They could also suggest when and where policymakers should focus intervention efforts.

Network Disruption

Interrupting the flow of people, money and other components of trafficking is critical to identifying trafficking networks, disrupting their infrastructure at the source and eliminating them.

Unfortunately, network interruption requires the cooperation of authorities and the public surrounding the network. In some countries, such as Nepal and Costa Rica, officials are threatened or bribed into ignoring or otherwise allowing human trafficking. There is often inadequate regulatory oversight of industries known to use trafficked laborers. Traffickers can easily fabricate or alter a victim's identification documents, rendering them invisible to overburdened authorities.

To help authorities identify trafficking operations to target, researchers could turn to network analysis, a mathematical way of representing real world systems and their interactions. For example, network analysis can be used to map out the dynamics of users and their connections embedded in social networks, such as Facebook and Twitter. This can possibly identify at-risk persons or, alternatively, traffickers or customers.

Social network analysis could also help to determine which contacts have a critical influence over others. This may enable early identification of either a victim or trafficking transaction.

Human trafficking is a serious crime and an appalling violation of human rights. Almost every country is affected by human trafficking as a source of victims, a transit point, or a destination and location of abuse. These new mathematical tools show great potential both to interrupt the human trafficking cycle and to provide the information needed to help victims escape to safety.

Periodical and Internet Sources Bibliography

The following articles have been selected to supplement the diverse views presented in this chapter.

Sarah Brown, "Marriott International Launches Enhanced Human Trafficking Awareness Training," Marriott International, July 28, 2021. https://news.marriott.com/news/2021/07/28/marriott-international-launches-enhanced-human-trafficking-awareness-training.

Andrea Cipriano, "Can Technology Stop Human Trafficking?" Center On Media Crime and Justice, November 1, 2021. https://thecrimereport.org/2021/11/01/can-technology-stop-human-trafficking/.

Colin Daileda, "This Facial Recognition Technology Could Help Stop Online Child Trafficking," *Mashable*, June 28, 2017. https://mashable.com/article/facial-recognition-child-sex-trafficking.

Brittany Eastman, "Can Facial Recognition Software Within Transportation Technology Combat Modern Slavery and Human Trafficking?" *University of Michigan Law School Journal of Law and Mobility*, November 9, 2021. https://futurist.law.umich.edu/can-facial-recognition-software-within-transportation-technology-combat-modern-slavery-and-human-trafficking/.

Kylie Foy, "Turning Technology Against Human Traffickers," *MIT News*, May 6, 2021. https://news.mit.edu/2021/turning-technology-against-human-traffickers-0506.

Marco Gutierrez, "Crypto Kiosks Are Being Used for Human Trafficking and Drug Dealing, Federal Watchdog Warns," *Fortune*, January 11, 2022. https://fortune.com/2022/01/11/crypto-kiosks-human-drug-trafficking-gao-warns/.

Ted Knutson, "Crypto Increasingly Used in Human/Drug Trafficking Says GAO," *Forbes*, January 10, 2022. https://www.forbes.com/sites/tedknutson/2022/01/10/crypto-increasingly-used-in-humandrug-trafficking-says-gao/?sh=50e8a241637e.

Paul Payette, "Hotels Revamp Safety with Contactless Technologies," Nomadix, April 8, 2021. https://nomadix.com/hotels-revamp-safety-with-contactless-technologies/.

Cezary Podkul, "Human Trafficking's Newest Abuse: Forcing Victims into Cyberscamming," ProPublica, September 13, 2022. https://www.propublica.org/article/human-traffickers-force-victims-into-cyberscamming.

Alex J. Rouhandeh, "Hunting Sexual Predators: A Political Fight in Facial Recognition Legislature," *Newsweek*, March 2, 2021. https://www.newsweek.com/hunting-sexual-predators-political-fight-facial-recognition-legislation-1573303.

Michelle Russell, "The Dark Side of Contactless Check-In," PCMA, September 10, 2021. https://www.pcma.org/human-trafficking-contactless-check-in/.

Brian Shedd, "How Mobile Key Tech Could Help Combat Human Trafficking at Hotels," *Hospitality Technology*, July 23, 2019. https://hospitalitytech.com/how-mobile-key-tech-could-help-combat-human-trafficking-hotels.

Alex Whiting, "Tech Savvy Sex Traffickers Stay Ahead of Authorities as Lure Teens Online," Reuters, November 15, 2015. https://www.reuters.com/article/women-conference-traffickers/feature-tech-savvy-sex-traffickers-stay-ahead-of-authorities-as-lure-teens-online-idUKL8N1343ZL20151116.

Chapter 4

Can Human Trafficking Be Prevented?

Chapter Preface

The question of whether human trafficking can be prevented is a difficult one. Many people assert that it should be the responsibility of governments to find ways to effectively curb and punish human trafficking. But could governments around the world agree on what should be done? Is it even possible for a single nation's government to take on trafficking? In many cases trafficking is an international issue, with victims of trafficking coming from one country and being trafficked in another. Is it more effective to attempt to prevent someone from being drawn into trafficking to begin with, or is it only possible to apprehend traffickers once the crime has already taken place? How can the governments of different countries as well as independent organizations cooperate to make this happen?

Human trafficking is a complex issue, so not surprisingly, the attempts at prevention or even prosecution of convicted traffickers is not any easier. Ideas and strategies are suggested and tested. How can governments make inroads into this crime that some equate with modern slavery if victims don't always report the crime? Can governments change the minds of people who support forced marriages? And what about women who traffic other women and girls?

The viewpoints in this chapter investigate these questions and create an understanding of how these issues affect human trafficking. Viewpoints from Valentin Luz and Kelly Twedell highlight some of the challenges to stopping human trafficking, while Anita Teekah, William Sheehan, Coral Dando, and Corinne Schwarz help dispel some of the myths and stereotypes about how human trafficking happens in order to more effectively address it. Finally, Ruth Dearnley, Sarah Gallo, and Lumina Albert describe ways that human trafficking might be stopped.

> *"Anti-trafficking strategies have to be embedded in every policy area, from improving female education in source countries so that girls are less vulnerable to trafficking, to increasing police pay in destination countries so that officers are less susceptible to bribery."*

Steps to Prevent Human Trafficking

Ruth Dearnley

In the following viewpoint, Ruth Dearnley contends that today's human trafficking can be equated to modern slavery. Dearnley provides statistics that spotlight the worldwide phenomenon of trafficking and then outlines the programs that organizations like Stop the Traffik and the United Nations are using in their efforts to combat the illegal and immoral practice. She explains how human trafficking is related to other societal issues, including asylum and immigration, smuggling, and prostitution. Because immigration and prostitution are politically contentious issues, people who are forced into human trafficking can be stigmatized as a result. Ruth Dearnley has been the CEO of Stop the Traffik since 2008.

As you read, consider the following questions:

1. According to Dearnley, what is one of the first steps of trafficking prevention?
2. According to the author, approximately what percent of trafficking victims are under age 18?
3. As reported by this viewpoint, what is the connection between chocolate and human trafficking?

How much would you pay for a winter coat? How much would you pay for the child that made it?

Fifty years ago, the abomination of slavery seemed like a thing of the past. But history has a way of repeating itself. Today, we find that human slavery is once again a sickening reality. At this moment, men, women and children are being trafficked and exploited all over the world: 2.4 million have been trafficked into forced labour worldwide of these, 600,000 to 800,000 are trafficked across borders each year and 12,000 children are working as slaves on cocoa plantations in West Africa. It is impossible to ever reach a consensus on the true scale of the problem but, regardless of the figures, what matters is that human trafficking is big and getting bigger. What matters is that every number represents a human life destroyed. It is happening on every continent and in almost every country: whether the place we live is a source, destination or transit point for trafficking, none of us can claim to be wholly unaffected by this crime.

As the extent of human trafficking is recognized, a number of approaches to tackling it have been developed. Stop the Traffik is one such approach. Born out of witnessing first-hand the effects of human trafficking, we started out in 2006 as an informal coalition dedicated to raising awareness of trafficking and generating the political will necessary to stop it.

During our short existence we have found that one of the biggest impediments to anti-trafficking efforts is a lack of understanding of the issue. Trafficking, and consequently, the measures taken to combat it, is often entangled with people smuggling, immigration and asylum, prostitution and other forms of organized crime. It must be emphasized that the essence of trafficking is the forced exploitation of individuals by those in the position to exert power over them. While moving people is an intrinsic part of trafficking, this may occur within as well as across borders, and it may take a variety of forms. If they have been tricked or deceived, a person may even willingly transport themselves into a situation of exploitation. But unlike those who pay to be smuggled into another country, victims of trafficking have no prospect of making a new life for themselves.

International trafficking will inevitably raise issues of immigration, but its victims cannot simply be treated as illegal migrants, nor can the efforts to tackle it be reduced to stricter border controls. We can find sex trafficking abhorrent without taking a particular stance against prostitution, and policies to reduce or control the sex industry are just one approach to ending the trade of human flesh. Finally, despite the similarities between the organized trafficking of drugs, arms and humans, which may require comparable police tactics to combat, we commit a grave injustice against the victims of human slavery if we reduce them in our minds to the status of commodities.

The first step to preventing human trafficking and prosecuting the traffickers is therefore to recognize the complexity of the crime which cannot be tackled in a vacuum. Anti-trafficking strategies have to be embedded in every policy area, from improving female education in source countries so that girls are less vulnerable to trafficking, to increasing police pay in destination countries so that officers are less susceptible to bribery. We cannot allow ourselves to marginalize the issue of trafficking, viewing it as something that can be ended with a few extra taskforces or dedicated units. We need everyone to be aware of how it affects them, and what they can do to stop it. Laudable efforts in this direction have already been made. In 2000, the United Nations launched the Protocol to Prevent, Suppress and Punish Trafficking in Persons, which established a victim-centred approach to trafficking. It has since been signed by 177 countries. In 2005, the Council of Europe Convention on Action against Trafficking in Human Beings marked a step towards greater cooperation and dedication within Europe.

But more needs to be done. Many people still do not know what trafficking is, or do not care. We are working to change that, at every level of society. In February 2008 we delivered 1.5 million signatures to the UN from people calling for an end to human trafficking; as a result, our founder Steve Chalke was appointed UN.GIFT Special Advisor on Community Action against Human Trafficking. Since then we have continued to build on our grassroots support, firm in the belief that trafficking cannot be stopped by international conventions alone. Our focus is currently geared towards three key campaigns.

First is Start Freedom, our dynamic new global project run in conjunction with the UN that aims to engage and raise awareness among young people, helping them learn about the issues surrounding human trafficking. The fact that over half of all victims of human trafficking are under 18 empowers young people to realize the importance of their potential to prevent this illicit trade. Already we've had stories from source, transit and destination countries such as Greece, Mexico and Nepal, about how young people, schools, faith groups and communities are engaging with Start Freedom. Communities are at the heart of our campaigns. During Freedom Week in March 2010, young people will connect, engage and share in their communities varied and creative ways to mark their objection to human trafficking.

Our other key project at the moment is Active Communities against Trafficking (ACT), which aims to bring together members of a community under the umbrella of an ACT group. We equip these groups with an abundance of resources to help them identify trafficking, understand how it affects local communities, and learn how to help prevent its continuation. They can do this by asking questions about missing children and by forming connections with local authorities, professionals and community leaders. We believe trafficking starts in a community, and can be stopped by a community, and as the ACT project takes hold across countries, we are witnessing the profile of trafficking being raised, bringing together a diversity of people to help combat human trafficking in its various guises. The second stage of ACT, currently being piloted, will be launched in 2010. It is essentially a community research project that aims to gather information about human trafficking for sexual exploitation in local communities. This project has strong potential to contribute immensely to our key objectives: prevention of trafficking, prosecution of traffickers and protection of victims.

A third central focus is our Chocolate Campaign, which is informed by the fact that more than a third of the world's cocoa comes from Côte d'Ivoire, where child trafficking and forced labour has been widely documented and acknowledged by international initiatives, such as the International Cocoa Initiative. Since international deadlines for eradicating child trafficking were missed by manufacturers, we decided to campaign ourselves by trying to get the big chocolate manufacturers to tell us that their products are "traffik free". Up until very recently, most of them could not guarantee this—quite simply because their supply chains were not free of child slavery. Our Chocolate Campaign encourages people to help spread awareness about child trafficking in the cocoa industry, and to pressurize big chocolate manufacturers to commit to certifications, such as Fair Trade or Rainforest Alliance, which are currently the best guarantees we have to indicate that products are "traffik free". Our campaign strategy relies on our numerous grassroots supporters: people host Fair Trade Chocolate Fondue fundraisers, send letters and make phone calls to manufacturers, boycott brands until they become Fair Trade, and hold awareness-raising events to inform and empower others to make ethical decisions. Our successes so far have been fantastic: Cadbury committed to a Fair Trade Dairy Milk, and Mars promised to certify the Galaxy bar with the Rainforest Alliance by 2010, and their whole range by 2020. Within a few weeks of targeting Nestlé to commit to a fair trade Kit Kat, we got news that they too were following suit in the United Kingdom by introducing a Fairtrade four-finger Kit Kat in January. This is a start, but it is nowhere near the end.

Only with a concerted effort by governments, private companies, non-governmental organizations, and above all communities, can we hope to end the horror of human trafficking. Stop the Traffik has developed into an independent charity with over 1,500 member organizations and hundreds of thousands of individuals around the world who refuse to tolerate the existence of slavery in the twenty-first century.

People are talking, communities are rising, global networks are being forged and governments are responding to the united message that human trafficking must end.

> *"Perhaps one of the more contemporary examples of female criminality where victims are also females is the trafficking of women for sexual exploitation."*

What Causes Women to Traffic Other Women?

Coral Dando

In the following viewpoint, Coral Dando presents an argument about the issue of female criminality and its role in human trafficking. Dando cites well-known cases of women who committed notorious crimes, while later delving into the issues of coercion and women's roles as both victims and offenders. Dando maintains that female criminality is a complicated problem. In many cases these women were victimized and exploited in the past and may be trying to escape further victimization. However, sometimes they are simply motivated by the economic opportunities trafficking presents. Coral Dando is a professor of forensic psychology at the University of Westminster in London.

As you read, consider the following questions:

1. Do women or men commit more crimes, according to Dando?

"Why Do Women Sex Traffic Other Women and Girls?" by Coral Dando, Psychology Today LLC, July 24, 2020. Reprinted by permission.

2. What percentage of traffickers are women, as reported in the viewpoint?
3. Is female criminality a clear-cut issue, as represented by the author?

The statistics are stark, consistent, and largely unambiguous: Women commit far less crime than men and have lower rates of arrest and prosecution than men for all types of crime, apart from prostitution.

Not surprisingly, worldwide, the numbers of women in prison are small versus men, which may be why when females are accused and convicted of involvement in serious crime, their cases attract considerable coverage, commentary, and debate—often far more than equivalent examples of male offending, and even more so when the victims of female criminals are also female.

There are numerous instances where the perpetrator and victim are both female. Some of the most well-known are where mothers have killed and/or seriously assaulted female children and stepchildren, and where female carers (e.g., nurses and childminders) have murdered and/or assaulted female children in their care.

For example, in the U.K., Rosemary West was convicted in 1995 of killing her stepdaughter, and in 1993, nurse Beverley Allitt was convicted of murdering and attempting to murder female and male babies in her care. In the U.S., Andrea Yates confessed to drowning her five children, one of whom was female (although this murder conviction was later overturned). In 2004, Dena Schlosser amputated the arms of her daughter, who later died. Other examples include female suicide bombers and women who have played a significant role in terrorist organisations such as Al-Qaeda, the Black Widows, and Hamas.

Perhaps one of the more contemporary examples of female criminality where victims are also females is the trafficking of women for sexual exploitation. Human trafficking is a serious organised crime where people (women and men) are transported from one part of a country to another and/or from one country to another, using violence, threats of violence, deception, and coercion. Upon arrival, victims are then exploited for financial or personal gain, including sexual exploitation.

Worldwide, conviction rates for human trafficking are negligible, but the numbers of women convicted are at odds with the statistical trends of female offending. In 2012, the United Nations Global Report on Trafficking in Persons highlighted that while a high number of trafficking victims were female, there was also a high rate of female offenders.

In Australia, for instance, between 2004 and 2017, there were only 20 convictions for human trafficking, nine of which were female. Worldwide, 38 percent of the suspected perpetrators of human trafficking are female, with women from central Europe and East Asia twice as likely to be suspected of human trafficking than men (68 percent versus 32 percent). In the U.K., the first person convicted under the modern slavery laws introduced in 2015 was female—she had trafficked females from Nigeria to Germany to work as sex slaves. Most recently, Ghislaine Maxwell has been charged with the enticement of minors and sex trafficking of young girls, apparently for her boyfriend Jeffrey Epstein and possibly for other adult men, although she denies the charges.

The known female prison population is low—for example, representing approximately 4 percent of the prison population in the U.K., and generally reducing worldwide. So, this apparently emerging trend of female protagonists in the trafficking of women has raised a series of psychological questions centred on coercion and control.

Are female perpetrators in similar circumstances to their victims, or are they are willing agents in this particular type of criminal activity? The answers to these questions are far from clear, but we know from other contexts just how insidious and effective psychological coercion and control can be. Research by the prison reform trust found that just under half of women prisoners reported having been coerced into committing offences to support someone else's drug use. Many imprisoned female foreign nationals are known to have been coerced or trafficked into offending, and it is not unusual for women to state they had offended to "keep their man."

However, victim representations of female offenders as powerless and controlled by men are challenged by many because this ignores that some women may see criminal activity as an easy way of improving their situation. Victim-offenders are offenders with a history of victimisation—and in the context of human trafficking, this concept goes some way towards helping to understand the victim/offender nexus. A critical time for a trafficked woman is when she has cleared any debt. At this point, some women are known to transition to offenders, choosing to stay and work in the sex trafficking industry, driven by a desire for improved economic opportunity and a better quality of life.

What is clear is that classifying female criminals as victims OR offenders ignores the victim-offender nexus and seems to underestimate the complexity of a lot of female criminality. In the U.K., progress has been made in cases of domestic violence. In the context of human trafficking, there appears little impetus to alter the victim OR offender dichotomy, which has implications for how female victim-offenders are perceived and judged by society and criminal justice systems, worldwide. It may be that these women are simply bad—sociopaths or psychopaths, perhaps. But perhaps they are being twice-punished.

Viewpoint 3

> *"Because forced marriage happens as a result of various threats, pressure, or coercion, where one or both participants do not or cannot consent, forced marriage is human trafficking."*

Forced Marriage Is Human Trafficking

Anita Teekah and William Sheehan

In the following viewpoint Anita Teekah and William Sheehan provide a definition of forced marriage and explain the difference between arranged marriages and forced marriages. The authors contend that forced marriage is in itself a form of human trafficking and that other types of trafficking can often occur because of forced marriages. Forced marriage occurs as a result of emotional or financial threats or coercion, and thus fits the standard definition of human trafficking. The authors explain how common forced marriage is and provide information on how to seek help. Anita Teekah is the senior director of anti-trafficking at Safe Horizon. William Sheehan is a staff attorney with the Safe Passage Project.

As you read, consider the following questions:

1. According to the viewpoint, what is the definition of forced marriage?

"Forced Marriage Is Human Trafficking: We Explain How and Why," by Anita Teekah and William Sheehan, Safe Horizon, December 11, 2019. Reprinted by permission.

2. According to the authors, is an arranged marriage the same as forced marriage?
3. What are two other types of trafficking that can occur because of forced marriage, as reported in this viewpoint?

Safe Horizon's Anti-Trafficking Program (ATP) is dedicated to supporting survivors of all forms of human trafficking in New York City. As one of the largest direct service providers to victims of human trafficking on the east coast, we recognize that forced marriage is a form of human trafficking and are working to raise awareness of this issue that affects 15.4 million globally (Global Estimates of Modern Slavery: Forced Labour and Forced Marriage, the International Labor Organization, 2016).

In this blog post, we explain forced marriage and how it is considered human trafficking so that more people and service providers will be able to identify survivors and offer support.

What Is Forced Marriage?

Marriage is the legal or formal recognition of the union of two consenting people in a personal relationship. Forced marriage is when one or both participants are married without consent. Forced marriage happens as a result of emotional and financial threats, pressure, or coercion. Therefore, usually one or both participants do not have the chance or power to consent.

Are Arranged Marriages a Form of Forced Marriages?

An arranged marriage is a common tradition in many cultures. It is not the same as forced marriage. In an arranged marriage, two families may play a role to set up and marry their children, but ultimately, those entering into marriage make the choice to freely do so. An arranged marriage becomes a forced marriage when one or both individuals are denied the ultimate decision to marry or not.

Why Is Forced Marriage Defined as Human Trafficking?

All types of human trafficking involve force, fraud, and coercion. The Trafficking Victims Protection Act (TVPA) of 2000 is legislation that defines and criminalizes human trafficking. Forced marriage is considered involuntary servitude under the TVPA's definition of human trafficking. The TVPA defines involuntary servitude as a "condition of servitude induced by means of any scheme, plan, or pattern intended to cause a person to believe that, if the person did not enter into or continue in such condition, that person or another person would suffer serious harm or physical restraint; or the abuse or threatened abuse of the legal process." Because forced marriage happens as a result of various threats, pressure, or coercion, where one or both participants do not or cannot consent, forced marriage is human trafficking.

Additional Abuse in Forced Marriage and Human Trafficking

Victims of forced marriage can also experience sex trafficking and/or labor trafficking. Sex trafficking is the performance of a commercial sexual act under threat of force, fraud or coercion. Labor trafficking is the performance of labor or services also through the use of force, fraud, or coercion.

For example, one of our clients is a woman who was forced to marry someone from abroad. After she was forced into marriage, she was threatened by her husband to perform sex acts for money. Therefore, she was a victim of both forced marriage and sex trafficking.

Forced marriage can also include more traditional forms of labor trafficking, such as physical work inside and outside the home. For example, if a woman is coerced into marrying a man who forces her to work at his family's restaurant, then she is a victim of both forced marriage and labor trafficking, both of which are types of human trafficking.

How Common Is Forced Marriage and Human Trafficking?

As reported in the 2016 Global Estimates of Modern Slavery: Forced Labour and Forced Marriage, the International Labor Organization (ILO) stated:

- That at any given time in 2016, an estimated 40.3 million people were living in modern slavery. This includes 24.9 million in forced labor and 15.4 million in forced marriage.
- Women and girls are disproportionately affected by forced labor, accounting for 99% of victims in the commercial sex industry, and 58% in other sectors.

What Help Is Available for Someone in a Forced Marriage?

Safe Horizon's Anti-Trafficking Program offers comprehensive legal and social services to anyone who has been trafficked, including victims of forced marriage. If you or someone you know is in a forced marriage and would like to access support and services, please call our intake line at 718-943-8652. Help is available.

> *"For many survivors, reporting their human trafficking experience can be complicated and the judicial process can be lengthy and sometimes retraumatizing."*

Not All Trafficking Victims Report the Crime

Valentin Luz

In the following viewpoint, Valentin Luz provides an overview of human trafficking in Canada. Luz contends that there are misconceptions about this crime and gives examples of them. He also maintains that there are many reasons why a trafficking victim may choose not to report the crime against them, demonstrating that trafficking is a very complicated issue. Some of these reasons include that they may worry that disclosing would put them in danger, that they are afraid of getting in legal trouble if they go to the police, and that they have a relationship with their trafficker. At the time this viewpoint was published, Valentin Luz served as a coordinator at the Canadian Centre to End Human Trafficking.

As you read, consider the following questions:

1. According to Luz, what is one reason that trafficking victims might not report this crime?
2. How long does it typically take to process a trafficking crime in Canada, as reported in this viewpoint?

"Why Victims and Survivors of Human Trafficking May Choose Not to Report," by Valentin Luz, The Canadian Centre to End Human Trafficking, November 18, 2020. Reprinted by permission.

3. Are traffickers typically strangers to those they traffic, according to the author?

When it comes to reporting human trafficking offenses to law enforcement, very few victims and survivors of both sex and labour trafficking choose to report, despite human trafficking being a criminal offence in Canada. For many survivors, reporting their human trafficking experience can be complicated and the judicial process can be lengthy and sometimes retraumatizing.

Choosing to report can also be empowering for survivors: it is one way to give voice to an experience and hold a trafficker accountable. Each person's story is their own and they are entitled to make the choice about whether or not they report. Below, we discuss several factors which may impact someone's decision to report to law enforcement.

Please note, this post is not intended to discourage reporting to police but rather to raise awareness of the many complex and unique considerations for survivors when it comes to reporting their trafficking experience.

Misconceptions About Human Trafficking

Human trafficking is often wrongly associated as only a crime against children, as something that only happens in other countries, or something that includes abduction and more closely resembles the Hollywood movie *Taken* with Liam Neeson. Unfortunately, these misconceptions shape the responses of service providers, law enforcement and the public to the crime and negatively affect society's collective capacity to identify victims of trafficking and understand their experiences. Finally, misconceptions may also lead to victims of trafficking not recognizing that what is happening to them is a in fact crime, and thus not reporting it.

Concerns for Safety

Traffickers may threaten victims, their families and loved ones with physical harm and abuse if they report their exploitation.

Fear of Reprimand for Associated Crimes

Traffickers may force or require a victim to commit other crimes such as theft and drug related offenses. In some cases, a trafficker may demand that the victim recruit others into human trafficking. This may deter some survivors from reporting to police due to a fear of being charged criminally. In situations where the victim is a foreign national in Canada, and lacks stable immigration status, the risk of deportation may also cause victims not to disclose their abuse. Click here for more information on the intersection of immigration status and the reporting of human trafficking.

Perceptions of Law Enforcement

Victims and survivors of human trafficking may not trust law enforcement, either because they themselves or their community have had past negative interactions with police, or because of lies they have been told by a trafficker, preventing once again a report to police. It is important to note that a mistrust in police, and the subsequent reluctance to report exploitation and abuse, disproportionately affects foreign nationals, LGBTQ2S, racialized and Indigenous peoples who come from communities with a history of conflict with law enforcement.

The Emotional Burden of the Judicial System

Statistics Canada reports that it takes approximately 358 days for a case involving human trafficking charges to go through the judicial system. This means that for up to a year, a survivor of human trafficking must be available emotionally and physically to the needs of the court process, bearing the responsibility of testifying and cross examination. Survivors are forced to retell the most traumatizing parts of their story, and often their memory of those moments and their character are questioned.

Additionally, in more cases than not, the judicial process does not result in a human trafficking conviction for the perpetrator, which can make survivors feel more unsafe and reluctant to report their situation to police.

Ending the Cycle of Human Trafficking

Human trafficking is a cycle. With a global economic crisis on the horizon, the demand for cheap labor is on the rise. People looking for jobs far from home are often deceived and tricked into forced labor or sexual exploitation. Many others are unemployed and living their lives in poverty. This places the poor at a higher risk of being trafficked, as victims of human trafficking are often poor, illiterate, and living under very serious health violations.

One of the incentives for trafficking is the huge profit made by the buyers and sellers, as well as the criminal organizations that keep the business going. In fact, human trafficking brings in billions of dollars in profit worldwide. Part of this money goes to South Africa, which has a GDP (Gross Domestic Product) of US$159.9 billion - four times larger than its neighboring countries. The trafficking of people brings in the third largest amount of money in the world, just behind drug and weapons dealing. But it is the uneven distribution of this money that continues to drive poverty and unemployment in Africa. Criminal organizations in South Africa use their profit to traffick more and more people overseas, as well as use some money for other areas of crime, including arms dealing and narcotics. In 2003, the children's institute at University of Cape Town stated that 75% of children in South Africa face poverty. As a result of human trafficking, poverty, unemployment, and inequality are all increasing.

As a result of human trafficking in Madagascar, The United States is looking to prevent the World Bank from financially supporting the country until it begins rebuilding the economy and taking steps towards the prevention of trafficking. The Bank does not want to be seen as a stimulant for such illicit activities. Madagascar continues to suffer from the economic effects of human trafficking, which include the lack of law enforcement, decrease in human productivity due to health conditions, and the circulation of money throughout the criminal organizations. When looking at human trafficking in retrospect, it must be brought to attention the fact that people are much easier to move across borders than any other trafficked items. Unlike many materialistic objects, human beings can be re-trafficked multiple times - thus making it an easy, low-risk business that continues to harm the economy of Madagascar.

"Human Trafficking: An Endless Cycle?" Human Trafficking Weebly.

Relationship with the Trafficker

Some survivors of human trafficking report being in an intimate relationship with their exploiter, may even share children together and live in the same dwelling. The survivor may also rely on the trafficker to have their basic needs met such as shelter and food. The bond between the trafficker and survivor makes it very challenging to press charges, even after they have left the relationship or exploitative situation. In some situations, the trafficker is a guardian or a relative, which can evoke confusing emotions of loyalty and love, and make it hard to report the crime.

Stigma and Shame of Disclosing

Victims and survivors of trafficking often experience stigma and shame as a result of their experiences. A common question asked is, 'why didn't you just leave?', but the process of human trafficking is complex and it can be incredibly confusing for victims and survivors to understand what has been done to them. Additionally, in some cultures, gender roles and stigma can add pressure, and reporting trafficking may carry significantly higher personal risk than trying to bury that experience and that trauma. It is also possible that a victim or survivor may feel that they consented to their exploitation or that the deserved the violence they experienced; traffickers are skilled at manipulation and making the victim feel responsible for the exploitation. No one can consent to being trafficked and no one 'deserves' to be trafficked.

> *"Fear, despair, and shame are just some of the reasons that trafficking victims may not seek help."*

Trafficking Victims Often Don't Ask for Help

Kelly Twedell

In the following viewpoint, Kelly Twedell analyzes the issue of getting help to victims of trafficking. Twedell explains that often trafficking victims may want help, but aren't sure how to go about getting it, or they might be afraid of being charged with crimes themselves. For systemic reasons and due to manipulation from their traffickers, trafficking victims are often isolated and unsure who to turn to for help. Twedell maintains that traffickers use techniques to control their victims, which puts up another barrier for victims seeking a way out of trafficking. Kelly Twedell is a co-founder of an anti-trafficking nonprofit 5 Sparrows, which was founded in 2012.

As you read, consider the following questions:

1. According to the author, do all people who are trafficked see themselves as victims?
2. What part does substance abuse play in the dilemma of non-reporting, as explained by Twedell?
3. How many instances of help may be needed to break the cycle of trafficking, as reported in the viewpoint?

"What Don't Victims Ask for Help? So Many Reasons," by Kelly Twedell, The Irina Project, December 12, 2018.

Based on the many harrowing news reports about human trafficking and sexual violence, one might wonder why victims don't just ask for help, or why they don't come forward to give impact statements to police upon an initial arrest during a sting operation. Society's long and shameful history of meeting claims of sexual violence with doubt and derision suggests at least one answer.

In fact, there are many barriers to seeking help. At 5 Sparrows in Cumberland County, North Carolina, we asked many of the 107 victims of sex and labor trafficking we served in 2017-2018 what were some of the obstacles to seeking and utilizing services. Following are some of the answers we have permission to share:

- "He is my boyfriend, and I'd get in trouble."
- "I thought I'd get arrested with the drugs."
- "I don't trust the police; sometimes they are the ones paying for my time."
- "He gives me some of the money, and I need it to pay bills."
- "What happens next to me?"
- "It's embarrassing."
- "I thought he would change, but it kept getting worse."
- "I lost hope."
- "He had a gun, and I was afraid."
- "He threatened to hurt my parents if I told."
- "I am part of this, and I don't want to go to jail."

These statements – evidencing fear, despair, and shame – are just some of the reasons that trafficking victims may not seek help. Researchers have noted the potent effects of psychological harm directed at victims by their traffickers. "This ingrained fear, lack of knowledge about alternatives, systemic isolation leading to a mistrust in others, and physical and psychological confinement is what causes many victims to be afraid to ask for help," wrote Gonzalez, Spencer and Smith in a 2017 study of the experiences of women exiting sex trafficking.

For service providers like us, of course, a first step is to identify victims. Often, in the screening process, we realize that a person does not understand they have been exploited. Some victims mistakenly believe they were complicit in their exploitation because they were in a romantic relationship with their trafficker. Others have told us, “I agreed to do this on my own; nobody is forcing me.” The myths about trafficking and the lies of the traffickers have to be unraveled before victims come to understand they were exploited for others’ personal gain.

Another barrier to seeking help is substance addiction. A 2014 study of the healthcare consequences of trafficking found that among 102 survivors, 84.3% reported they were alcohol or drug dependent while they were being trafficked. In the many victim testimonies we have heard, women said that drugs helped them ‘zone out’ from the sex work. Others said that drugs, mainly heroin and cocaine, helped them stay awake through the night to meet the quotas set for them by their traffickers.

Some victims become caught in the perpetual cycle of drug addiction while being exploited.

Understandably, they may fear they’ll be arrested for drugs “willfully” accepted as part of their “compensation” from the trafficker, when in fact the trafficker has likely used drugs as a means of controlling the victim. Fortunately, Cumberland County judges are educated about what trafficking looks like, and as a result they might choose to defer charges or grant a continuance in a case while a victim seeks treatment.

An extended restoration program can be part of a broader effort to provide trafficking victims with lasting results (as opposed to the quick-fix of being bonded out of jail). However, fear of the unknown discourages some victims from asking for help. Knowing there will be a five- to seven-day detox period from drugs and unsure whether they are safe in the community where they were victimized exacerbates feelings of insecurity. Some worry that victims who leave a detox program prematurely will disclose the names and locations of victims still in treatment. Others fear the prospect of being separated from children temporarily when they enter treatment, or of losing custody altogether.

The fact is, a person becomes ready to ask for and accept help in her own time (I say "her" because 96 percent of the victims we served at 5 Sparrows during this time were female or identified as female). An initial meeting with organizations like ours establishes for victims where we are and what we do. Sometimes, they contact us to begin the process of restoration, only to return to trafficking – it's not unusual for that cycle to repeat itself. In some cases, it has taken victims three to four attempts before they complete a restoration program and reintegrate with a healthier view on life and on themselves. Each person's healing journey looks different, and we respect that.

People are mistaken if they believe that trafficking victims do not want help – on the contrary, our experience shows that they want help, but they might not be sure what that looks like. Victim service organizations are in a position to start the conversation and illuminate the range of resources available to them without cost.

Sources

Nicole Gonzalez, Chelsea Spencer and Sandra Stith, "Moving to Restoration: The Experiences of Women Exiting Sex Trafficking," *Journal of Human Trafficking* (2017), advance online publication, https://doi.org/10.1080/23322705.2017.1413856

Laura J. Lederer and Christopher A. Wetzel, "The Health Consequences of Sex Trafficking and Their Implications for Identifying Victims in Healthcare Facilities," *The Annals of Health Law* 23 (2014): 61-91.

Viewpoint 

> *"Training can help employees recognize the signs of human trafficking, which can help stop it in its tracks."*

Companies Can Make a Difference in the Life of a Trafficking Victim

Sarah Gallo

In the following viewpoint, Sarah Gallo asserts that companies can help prevent or give aid to trafficking victims with the right type of training provided to their employees. Gallo explains that for the greatest effectiveness, the training should fit the specific industry and employees should be encouraged to get involved and understand that they may be saving the life of an individual. Often people feel like they don't want to get involved when they see signs of trafficking or feel like it's not their business, so a cultural change that encourages intervention is necessary. Sarah Gallo is an associate editor at Training Industry Inc. and co-hosts a podcast The Business of Learning.

As you read, consider the following questions:

1. What three industries are prone to trafficking, as reported in the viewpoint?

"Human Trafficking Awareness Training: How Companies Can Make a Difference," by Sarah Gallo, Training Industry, January 23, 2020. Reprinted by permission. The article was originally published on TrainingIndustry.com, https://trainingindustry.com/articles/compliance/human-trafficking-awareness-training-how-companies-can-make-a-difference.

2. What makes anti-trafficking training most valuable, according to the author?
3. As stated by Gallo, what are two signs that someone may be a trafficking victim?

According to the U.S. Department of Homeland Security, "Human trafficking involves the use of force, fraud, or coercion to obtain some type of labor or commercial sex act." Although it's difficult to determine the scope of human trafficking worldwide, as many cases go unreported, the International Labour Organization estimates that there were about 40.3 million victims of human trafficking international in 2016 alone. As January is Human Trafficking Awareness Month, let's look at how training can help organizations combat what is not only an organizational issue but a human one.

How Training Can Help

Training can help employees recognize the signs of human trafficking, which can help stop it in its tracks. For example, in 2016, an Uber driver was able to stop a teenage girl from being trafficked by recognizing the warning signs and immediately contacting law enforcement. Now, Uber partners with numerous organizations to "mobilize communities, raise awareness, and advocate for policy and legislation" and educates its drivers on how to identify and respond to human trafficking through training materials and in-person sessions in major cities such as Seattle, Baltimore and Sacramento.

Recognizing the active role training plays in combating human trafficking, many states have adopted human trafficking awareness training requirements—especially in industries particularly prone to trafficking, such as hospitality, transportation and manufacturing.

However, organizations across industries have a "shared responsibility" to combat human trafficking through training and awareness efforts, says Andrew Rawson, chief learning officer at

Traliant. "If we don't train people on these issues, then I don't know how, as a public, we can help identify and rescue [victims]."

Best Practices for Maximum Impact

To be effective, human trafficking awareness training should be tailored to the specific industry—or, better yet, job role—at hand. For example, Rawson recommends customizing training for housekeepers, front desk workers, food and beverage workers, and maintenance workers to provide learners with "practical examples" of what to look for. Ashley Garrett, director of the National Human Trafficking Training and Technical Assistance Center (NHTTAC) echoes the importance of industry-specific training, as warning signs are largely industry-dependent. For example, health care organizations should train employees to look for patients who defer to someone else when answering medical questions or who don't seem to have control over their documentation.

"I would encourage organizations or industries to look in the context of what their own workforce is, and who their own customer and consumer base is, to understand more specifically what their red flags are," Garrett says. Conducting risk assessments can help learning leaders identify these red flags and "understand how to step in and intervene."

Training programs should also address more general signs of human trafficking, such as people who look "incredibly distressed," unusually exhausted, paranoid and/or fearful or who seem to have no control over their money, travel documentation and/or other forms of identification, says Dr. Mar Brettman, chief executive officer of Businesses Ending Slavery and Trafficking (BEST).

Once employees understand how to recognize human trafficking, they need training on how to respond, whether it's bringing concerns to a manager's attention or, in more urgent cases, contacting law enforcement or the National Human Trafficking Hotline. "The easy part is teaching people what to look for," Rawson says. The hard part, however, is encouraging employees to take action, as many "don't want to get involved."

Leaders should encourage employees to "come up the chain of command" with any human trafficking-related concerns they may have, Rawson adds. Further, bystander intervention training can equip employees with the tools they need to feel confident speaking up after identifying signs of human trafficking.

Supporting Human Trafficking Survivors

"Survivors are coming out of their experience wanting to thrive, and one of the things that they want, and need, are employment opportunities," Garrett says. Through professional development opportunities, organizations can support human trafficking survivors in a achieving their career goals. To set survivors up for professional success, BEST partnered with Waldron Consulting to provide workshops on basic career skills, such as how to build a resume and how to interview.

Partnering with local victim services organizations is another way companies can help build "supportive career pathways" for human trafficking survivors, says Sarah Gonzalez Bocinski, program manager of Future Without Violence's economic justice and workforce initiatives. That organization's "Promoting Employment for Survivors of Trafficking" (PEOST) project builds "strong collaborations" between victim services agencies and workforce development programs to improve survivors' "access to quality education, training and employment opportunities."

To truly make a difference, organizations must first understand the prevalence and impact of all types of trauma and work to dismantle the obstacles they create that can hinder survivors' access to employment. "This means adopting a human-centered approach to work that is more collaborative and supportive, rather than transactional," Gonzalez Bocinski says.

The Bottom Line

In addition to the more urgent impact trafficking has on its human victims, it can also cause numerous issues for employers, including a tarnished company brand, liability issues and decreased productivity. Training can help combat these issues—and help employees feel inspired to continue working at a "company that cares" and that exercises corporate responsibility.

However, the true bottom line is simple: Many victims of human trafficking have no one advocating for them, Rawson says. "That's why it's particularly important that organizations provide this training on human trafficking … whether it's required by law or not." After all, the training is relatively brief and inexpensive to deliver, but it has the potential to save lives. In terms of value, that's one benefit that simply can't be measured.

Viewpoint 7

> *"Schools can play an important role in helping students learn about and protect themselves from human trafficking."*

Schools Can Help Stop Human Trafficking

Lumina Albert

In this viewpoint, Lumina Albert argues that educators can help teach students the risks of human trafficking and watch for signs of human trafficking. Formal training can help school staff learn how to do this, and this viewpoint outlines the five key goals that all anti-trafficking educational programs should keep in mind. These include creating a safe and welcoming environment for students, watching for triggers in students who have been exposed to trauma, and dispelling stereotypes and misconceptions about human trafficking. Lumina Albert is an associate professor of management and director of the CSU Center for Ethics and Human Rights at Colorado State University.

As you read, consider the following questions:

1. According to data cited in this viewpoint, what percent of human trafficking survivors were first trafficked before they turned 18?
2. At the time this viewpoint was published, what four states required human trafficking education in schools?

"Schools join the fight against human trafficking," by Lumina Albert, The Conversation, January 24, 2022. https://theconversation.com/schools-join-the-fight-against-human-trafficking-172749.

3. According to Albert, what are triggers?

Education leaders across the U.S. are trying to figure out how to effectively teach students about the risks and warning signs of human trafficking, which includes being forced into domestic servitude, commercial labor or sex work.

According to 2019 data gathered by the Polaris Project – a nonprofit that fights human trafficking, including sex trafficking – 24% of survivors reported that they were first trafficked before they turned 18.

In 2017, California became the first state to require human trafficking education for students and teachers. Tennessee, Florida and Virginia also now require school staff to receive formal training intended to stop human trafficking.

As cases of human trafficking continue to make headlines, similar prevention and education efforts are being made in schools across the country. Parents and community members in other states may also find similar efforts coming to their communities. As a scholar who studies business ethics – and as executive director of the Center for Ethics and Human Rights at Colorado State University – I recommend school leaders keep five key goals in mind when creating anti-trafficking educational programs.

1. Create a Safe Haven

Childhood researchers suggest that children need a safe haven where they can go when confronted with fear and threats. They also need a secure base, a place where they feel secure to explore the world around them.

Ideally, children's homes would serve these purposes. But schools can also provide safe havens and secure bases. Children who feel more secure are less vulnerable to predatory people, who often fake affection and provide a false sense of love as a tactic to lure kids into the world of human trafficking.

2. Pay Attention to Triggers

When being taught about human trafficking, it's possible that children's memories of past trauma might be triggered. Educators who are aware of this possibility are more likely to be better at protecting kids from being triggered, and better able to respond properly if it happens.

Many children have been exposed to trauma, such as neglect or abandonment; physical, sexual or psychological abuse; loss of a loved one; or refugee or war experiences. When these memories are triggered, children feel distressed and unsafe.

Triggers may include words, tone of voice, facial expressions, smells, feelings or postures that are embedded in a child's mind. And some can cause unexpected reactions in seemingly regular situations. For instance, a child whose abusive parent used to eat oranges may be triggered by the smell of an orange, and this memory may became linked with the abusive experience in the child's mind. Or a common nickname might have been used by an abuser and can be a trigger.

Often, these memories are not conscious ones, so the child may not understand why they feel distressed or overwhelmed, and yet they respond to the trigger as if they are facing a real threat.

3. Be Inclusive

When teachers show compassion, warmth and kindness to their students, students are more likely to develop a strong sense of belonging in the classroom space.

Without that sense of belonging, students might come to see themselves as unworthy of attention and love, which hurts their self-esteem and makes them more vulnerable to the influence of predators.

4. Dispel Misconceptions and Stereotypes

Young white women are often depicted in media as representative of trafficking victims, although women and girls of color experience high rates of trafficking.

Also, women of color who are forced to engage in sexual acts or labor are often stereotyped as deviants and treated with suspicion by officials and law enforcement.

And while boys are less commonly trafficking victims, they are still at risk of being trafficked. In addition, many human trafficking reports do not provide data on nonbinary or gender-nonconforming people.

Trafficking education materials work best when they accurately discuss who the perpetrators are. Effective anti-trafficking education teaches kids that traffickers are not just strangers or people belonging to another race or ethnicity. Traffickers are often friendly, charismatic, well-dressed and seemingly wealthy, and they may appear to be kind and warm. They may also be close family members and caregivers who exploit children in their care.

5. Use Appropriate Touch and Tone

Teachers often use touch and tone of voice to build connections with children. But many children who have experienced trauma are sensitive to touch and avoid it. Teachers who learn how to use touch in reassuring and affirming ways – such as an encouraging pat on the back, an occasional handshake, high-five or fist bump – can help build a sense of safety and security in the classroom, building trust with students and making them less likely to fall prey to traffickers.

Similarly, using consistent tones of voice that are calm, reassuring and firm can help students' development, engagement, learning and growth.

Schools can play an important role in helping students learn about and protect themselves from human trafficking. With these five concepts in mind, school leaders will be better prepared to help keep kids safe.

VIEWPOINT 8

"Reducing sex trafficking requires changes that might prevent it from occurring in the first place."

Dispelling Myths About Sex Trafficking Can Help Fight It

Corinne Schwarz

In this viewpoint, Corinne Schwarz argues that there are many misconceptions about sex trafficking and that these myths and stereotypes prevent people from knowing what to actually watch out for. Schwarz explains that sex trafficking includes any case that involves force, fraud, or coercion, as well as any and all sexual exchanges involving a minor. She also points out that most cases do not involve complete strangers, but people who are at least somewhat familiar to the victim. Often sex trafficking victims are people in unstable living situations—such as those who are unhoused—and are exploited by other people as they attempt to meet their basic needs. Corinne Schwarz is an assistant professor of gender, women's, and sexuality studies at Oklahoma State University.

"Sex trafficking isn't what you think: 4 myths debunked – and 1 real-world way to prevent sexual exploitation," by Corinne Schwarz, The Conversation, July 29, 2021. https://theconversation.com/sex-trafficking-isnt-what-you-think-4-myths-debunked-and-1-real-world-way-to-prevent-sexual-exploitation-158852.

As you read, consider the following questions:

1. According to Schwarz, what is the negative effect of frontline workers inconsistently defining "trafficking victim"?
2. According to data from Covenant House cited in this viewpoint, what percent of trafficking survivors surveyed were trafficked by immediate family members?
3. What does Schwarz suggest can be done to help prevent sex trafficking?

The idea that sex trafficking is an urgent social problem is woven into American media stories, from reports of Republican U.S. Rep. Matt Gaetz's alleged trafficking of teenage girls to debunked QAnon conspiracy theories about a sexual slavery ring run through online retailer Wayfair.

The common perception of sex trafficking involves a young, passive woman captured by an aggressive trafficker. The woman is hidden and waiting to be rescued by law enforcement. She is probably white, because, as the legal scholar Jayashri Srikantiah writes, the "iconic victim" of trafficking usually is depicted this way.

This is essentially the plot of the "Taken" movies, in which teenage Americans are kidnapped abroad and sold into sexual slavery. Such concerns fuel viral posts and TikTok videos about alleged but unproven trafficking in IKEA parking lots, malls and pizza shops.

This is not how sex trafficking usually occurs.

Since 2013, I have researched human trafficking in the midwestern U.S. In interviews with law enforcement, medical providers, case managers, victim advocates and immigration lawyers, I found that even these frontline workers inconsistently define and apply the label "trafficking victim" – especially when it comes to sex trafficking. That makes it harder for these professionals to get trafficked people the help they request.

So here are the facts and the law.

What Is Sex Trafficking?

The Victims of Trafficking and Violence Protection Act of 2000 provides the official legal definition for sex and labor trafficking in the United States.

It makes "trafficking in which a commercial sex act is induced by force, fraud, or coercion, or in which the person induced to perform such act has not attained 18 years of age" a federal crime.

In short, to legally qualify as sex trafficking, a sex act involving an adult must include "force, fraud, and coercion." This could look like someone – a family member, a romantic partner or a market facilitator colloquially described as a "pimp" or "madam" – physically abusing or threatening another adult into sex for money or resources.

With minors, any and all sexual exchanges – that is, trading sex for something of value like cash or food – are considered sex trafficking.

How Common Is Sex Trafficking?

Data on human trafficking is notoriously messy and difficult to measure. Survivors may be hesitant to disclose their exploitation out of fear of deportation, if they are undocumented, or arrest. That leads to underreporting.

One way to approximate how many people are being trafficked in the United States is to consult federal grant reports, as suggested by anti-trafficking nonprofit Freedom Network USA.

For example, the federal Office for Victims of Crime served 9,854 total clients – some of whom identified as trafficked, others who showed "strong indicators of trafficking victimization" – between July 2019 and June 2020. The Department of Health and Human Services Office on Trafficking in Persons served 2,398 trafficking survivors during the 2019 fiscal year.

Data from the same office also shows that 25,597 "potential victims" of sex and labor trafficking were identified through calls to the National Human Trafficking Hotline.

Again, this data is incomplete – if survivors have not accessed these particular resources or called these specific hotlines, they are not represented here.

What Does Sex Trafficking Look Like?

As with other sexual crimes, like rape, sex trafficking survivors often experience violence at the hands of someone they know, not a complete stranger.

A study from Covenant House New York, a nonprofit focused on homeless youth, found that 36% of the 22 trafficking survivors in their survey were trafficked by an immediate family member, like a parent. Only four reported "being kidnapped and held against his or her will."

Often, trafficking victims are younger transgender people or teens experiencing homelessness who exchange sex with others to meet their basic needs: shelter, economic stability, food and health care. Trafficking frequently looks like vulnerable people struggling to survive in a violent, exploitative world.

"They are creating sexual solutions to nonsexual problems," says San Francisco-based researcher Alexandra Lutnick.

Under U.S. law, these youth are trafficking victims, because of their age. But they may reject the label, preferring terms like "survival sex work" or "prostitution" to describe their experiences.

Trafficking victims engaged in survival sex may well be arrested rather than offered help like housing or health care. If they cannot prove "force, fraud, or coercion," or if they refuse to comply in a criminal investigation, they risk shifting from victim to criminal in the eyes of law enforcement. That can mean prostitution charges, felony offenses or deportation.

Such punishments are most commonly used against Black, Indigenous, queer, trans and undocumented sex-trafficking survivors. Black youth are disproportionately arrested for prostitution offenses, for example, even though legally any underage commercial sex is sex trafficking.

What Is the Difference Between Sex Work and Sex Trafficking?

Legally and in other meaningful ways, sex work and sex trafficking are different.

Sex work is consenting adults engaging in transactional sex. In almost all U.S. states, it is a criminal offense, punishable with fines and even jail sentences.

Sex trafficking is nonconsensual, and it is generally treated as a more severe crime.

Most sex workers' groups acknowledge that sex work is not inherently sex trafficking but that sex workers can face force, fraud and coercion because they work in a criminalized, stigmatized profession. Sex workers whose experiences meet the legal standards of trafficking may nonetheless fear disclosing that to police and risking arrest for prostitution.

Conversely, sex workers can be mistakenly labeled by police and advocates as "trafficked" and find themselves in the custody of law enforcement or social service agencies.

What Can Be Done?

Based on my research, reducing sex trafficking requires changes that might prevent it from occurring in the first place. That means rebuilding a stronger, supportive U.S. social safety net to buffer against poverty and housing insecurity.

In the meantime, trafficking victims would benefit from efforts by frontline workers to combat the racism, sexism and transphobia that stigmatizes and criminalizes victims who don't look as people expect – and are struggling to survive.

Periodical and Internet Sources Bibliography

The following articles have been selected to supplement the diverse views presented in this chapter.

Jamille Bigio, "U.S. Should Treat Human Trafficking as a National Security Threat, Urges New CFR Report," Council on Foreign Relations, June 10, 2021. https://www.cfr.org/news-releases/us-should-treat-human-trafficking-national-security-threat-urges-new-cfr-report.

Ximena Bustillo, "A Human-Trafficking Case Exposed Farmworker Abuses. The Government Is Promising Change," NPR, May 27, 2022. https://www.npr.org/2022/05/27/1101741366/human-trafficking-farmworker-abuse-georgia.

Monica Dean, "Women Luring Women into Sex Trade Is Not Uncommon," NBC, May 4, 2017. https://www.nbcsandiego.com/news/local/women-luring-women-into-sex-trade-san-diego/14175/.

Paula Duhatschek, "Romeo Pimps: Sex Traffickers Luring Young Women by Posing as Potential Boyfriends, Experts Say," CBC, September 10, 2019. https://www.cbc.ca/news/canada/kitchener-waterloo/sex-trafficking-survivor-speaks-out-about-romeo-pimps-1.5272368.

Jacey Fortin, "Flight Attendants Fight Human Trafficking with Eyes in the Sky," *New York Times*, February 7, 2017. https://www.nytimes.com/2017/02/07/us/flight-attendants-human-trafficking.html.

Natalie Jesionka, "What's Being Done to Stop Human Trafficking?" the *Muse*, June 19, 2020. https://www.themuse.com/advice/whats-being-done-to-stop-human-trafficking.

Mark P. Lagon, "The US Government Turns a Blind Eye to Policies that Fuel Sex Trafficking," the *Washington Post*, February 1, 2016. https://www.washingtonpost.com/opinions/the-us-government-turns-a-blind-eye-to-policies-that-fuel-sex-trafficking/2016/02/01/959352e2-c6c6-11e5-a4aa-f25866ba0dc6_story.html.

James Lankford, "Getting the US Government Out of Human Trafficking for Good," the *Hill*, January 13, 2022. https://thehill.com/blogs/congress-blog/politics/589586-getting-the-us-government-out-of-human-trafficking-for-good/.

Matthew Lee, "US Hits 17 Nations for Not Combating Human Trafficking," PBS, July 1, 2021. https://www.pbs.org/newshour/politics/u-s-hits-17-nations-for-not-combating-human-trafficking.

Kelly McLaughlin, "A Shocking 38% of Sex Trafficking Suspects are Women—and Many are Former Victims," *Insider,* August 23, 2019. https://www.insider.com/women-play-a-large-role-in-sex-trafficking-operations-2019-8.

For Further Discussion

Chapter 1

1. After reading the viewpoints from Chapter 1, what do you think are some of the biggest causes of human trafficking?
2. Should the rich and powerful who engage in trafficking pay a heavier price for their crimes? Why or why not?
3. What role does political or societal unrest play in human trafficking?

Chapter 2

1. What could be done to make human trafficking a less lucrative business for traffickers?
2. The viewpoint by Brian Monroe analyzes how banks can deter trafficking. Do the suggestions seem enforceable? Explain your reasoning.
3. According to the viewpoints in this chapter, how do banks and charities team up to help human trafficking victims?

Chapter 3

1. According to the viewpoints in this chapter, what role does social media and the Internet play in human trafficking?
2. Based on the information in this chapter, what could be done to prevent human trafficking on the Internet?
3. What are some ways in which technology helps prevent human trafficking?

Chapter 4

1. Ruth Dearnley contends that communities need to be involved in stopping human trafficking. What kinds of efforts could be used in your community to prevent or stop trafficking?

2. Arranged marriages are an integral part of some cultures. How is arranged marriage different from forced marriage? Is there a clear-cut difference between the two, or might there be some overlap?
3. What are some of the difficulties trafficking victims face in reporting their traffickers?

Organizations to Contact

The editors have compiled the following list of organizations concerned with the issues debated in this book. The descriptions are derived from materials provided by the organizations. All have publications or information available for interested readers. The list was compiled on the date of publication of the present volume; the information provided here may change. Be aware that many organizations take several weeks or longer to respond to inquiries, so allow as much time as possible.

Anti-Slavery International

The Stableyard
Broomgrove Road
London, SW9 9TL
United Kingdom
+44 (0) 20 7737 9434
email: info@antislavery.org
website: www.antislavery.org

Anti-Slavery International is an organization dedicated to eradicating modern-day slavery (another term used for human trafficking). Learn about trafficking by reading the organization's blog and articles.

Department of Homeland Security

2707 Martin Luther King Jr. Avenue
Washington, DC 20528
(202) 282-8000
website: www.dhs.gov

The Department of Homeland Security has a mission to safeguard the U.S. and the American people. It is the department of the U.S. government responsible for public security. Human trafficking is one of this agency's topics of interest. Get information via fact sheets, blogs, and press releases, and learn about the Blue Campaign, a program to educate about human trafficking.

Federal Bureau of Investigation (FBI)

26 Federal Plaza, 23rd Floor
New York, NY 10278
(202) 324-3000
website: www.fbi.gov

The stated mission of the FBI is to protect the American people and uphold the Constitution of the United States. As the premier law enforcement agency of the United States, it maintains active online information about crime including human trafficking.

National Center for Missing and Exploited Children (NCMEC)

333 John Carlyle Street, Suite 125
Alexandria, VA 22314
(703) 224-2150
website: www.missingkids.org

The NCMEC is the largest and most influential child protection service in the United States. Its website contains a large amount of information about child trafficking.

National Human Trafficking Hotline

1 (888) 373-7888
email: help@humantraffickinghotline.org
website: https://humantraffickinghotline.org

The National Human Trafficking Hotline is a safe space for trafficking victims and survivors. The website includes statistics, resources, and information about safety planning.

Polaris Project

P.O. Box 65323
Washington, DC 20035
(202) 790-6300
website: https://polarisproject.org

This agency is dedicated to the understanding of human trafficking. Learn how to recognize human trafficking, and the myths, statistics, facts, and policy surrounding this issue on its website.

Stop the Traffik UK

35-41 Lower Marsh
London, SE1 7RL
United Kingdom
+44 (0) 207 921 4258
email: info@stopthetraffik.org
website: www.stopthetraffik.org

Stop the Traffik UK was founded in 2005 as a coalition to end trafficking worldwide. The organization's website includes reports on human trafficking and information about how to stop it.

UNICEF USA

125 Maiden Lane
New York, NY 10038
1 (800) 367-5437
website: www.unicefusa.org/mission/protect/trafficking

UNICEF is an organization dedicated to the well-being of children. Its page on child trafficking includes stories on what UNICEF is doing about human trafficking in the United States. It also includes information about what individuals can do to help.

United Way

701 Fairfax Street
Alexandria, VA 22314
(703) 836-7112
website: www.unitedway.org

United Way seeks to enhance the common good worldwide by bringing people together in its mission. Besides learning about trafficking and many other issues, this site provides suggestions and ways to get involved for doing good.

U.S. Department of State

2201 C Street NW
Washington, DC 20520
1 (888) 407-4747
website: www.state.gov

The U.S. Department of State is a governmental agency dedicated to the safety and prosperity of U.S. citizens. Use the search function to obtain links to valuable research and up-to-date information about human trafficking.

Bibliography of Books

Nita Belles. *In Our Backyard: Human Trafficking in America and What We Can Do to Stop It.* Grand Rapids, MI: Baker Books, 2015.

Julie K. Brown. *Perversion of Justice: The Jeffrey Epstein Story.* New York, NY: Dey Street, 2021.

Mary C. Burke, ed. *Human Trafficking: Interdisciplinary Perspectives* (Criminology and Justice Studies). 3rd ed. New York, NY: Routledge, 2022.

Mansi Choksi. *The Newlyweds: Rearranging Marriage in Modern India.* New York, NY: Atria Books, 2022.

Leanne K. Currie-McGhee. *Human Rights in Focus: Human Trafficking.* San Diego, CA: Reference Point Press, 2018.

Eamon Doyle, ed. *The Dark Web* (Current Controversies). New York, NY: Greenhaven Publishing, 2019.

Matthew S. Friedman. *Where Were You?: A Profile of Modern Slavery.* New York, NY: Penguin Books, 2021.

Dylan Howard. *Epstein: Dead Men Tell No Tales: Spies, Lies, & Blackmail.* New York, NY: Skyhorse Publishing Company, 2019.

Siddharth Kara. *Modern Slavery: A Global Perspective.* New York, NY: Columbia University Press, 2017.

Maggy Krell. *Taking Down Backpage: Fighting the World's Largest Sex Trafficker.* New York, NY: New York University Press, 2022.

Sara Kruzan. *I Cried to Dream Again: Trafficking, Murder, and Deliverance, A Memoir.* New York, NY: Pantheon Books, 2022.

Alexandra Lutnick. *Domestic Minor Sex Trafficking: Beyond Victims and Villains.* New York, NY: Columbia University Press, 2016.

Kathryn Roberts, ed. *Violence Against Women* (Global Viewpoints). New York, NY: Greenhaven Publishing, 2018.

Lita Sorenson, ed. *Human Trafficking* (Global Viewpoints). New York, NY: Greenhaven Publishing, 2019.

Wendy Stickle, Shelby Hickman, and Christine White. *Human Trafficking: A Comprehensive Exploration of Modern Day Slavery*. Los Angeles, CA: SAGE Publications, 2019.

Index

H

I

M

N

O

P

S